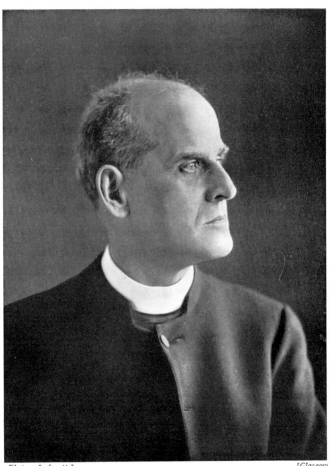

Yours very Sincerely

John White.

DR. JOHN WHITE

A BIOGRAPHY AND A STUDY

By

ALEXANDER GAMMIE

AUTHOR OF
"DR. GEORGE H. MORRISON : HIS LIFE AND WORK," ETC.

With Seven Illustrations on Art Paper

LONDON
JAMES CLARKE & CO., LIMITED
9, ESSEX STREET, STRAND, W.C. 2

"GREAT CHURCHMEN" SERIES

PRINTED IN GREAT BRITAIN

PREFACE

I DESIRE to thank the Rev. William White, B.D., Crosshouse ; the Rev. Robert H. Kerr, M.A., Canonbie ; and the Rev. Andrew Campbell, M.A., Crieff, for helpful information, and also (in connection with the history of the Barony Church) the Rev. John M. Munro, B.D., Strathbungo, Glasgow.

My thanks are also due to Sir Robert Horne, M.P., Professor Ernest F. Scott, New York ; and Dr. Archibald Fleming, St. Columba's, Pont Street, London, for their contributions which appear in these pages.

To Dr. White himself I am deeply indebted. While he has no responsibility for this volume, he has afforded me many special facilities with the courtesy and consideration which I have always experienced at his hands.

A. G.

GLASGOW.
August, 1929.

CONTENTS

LIST OF ILLUSTRATIONS

CHAPTER I

INTRODUCTORY

DR. JOHN WHITE has been described as "a philosopher in action," and the story of his career is a remarkable illustration of the truth of this estimate. By common consent he is acknowledged to be the greatest ecclesiastical statesman of his time in Scotland. And his fame has spread even beyond the bounds of his own land, for his great work as the Apostle of the reunion of Scottish Presbyterianism has attracted the attention of all the churches throughout the world, and has even touched the imagination of the general public. The movement of which he has been so largely the driving force, as well as the leading figure, has been so far reaching in its issues as to make it something more than a mere ecclesiastical development. It has assumed a national importance with a significance for the country as well as for the Church to which no lover of his native land can remain indifferent.

Only a man of action could have been the leader of such a movement ; and it should be interesting to trace how Dr. White, one of the most distinguished students of his time, was drawn forth from the seclusion of his study to play his part in the world of affairs. One can quite imagine that if he had been left quietly to pursue his studies he would have enriched the literature of philosophy and theology. But it was willed otherwise. The man who might have been making books has been making history.

It is the case that for every great hour the great man necessary is raised up by Providence to play his part. Never was this more strikingly exemplified than in the case of Dr. White. It will be shown in these pages how he was being prepared and fitted from the very first for what was ultimately to be the supreme work of his life. By the inheritance he received from his ancestry and by the atmosphere in which he was reared, he was being singularly equipped, although this fact may not as yet be generally known, for becoming the mediating influence between the two leading branches of Presbyterianism in Scotland. So also by the situation he was called upon to face at a very early stage in his career, in the first parish he served, was he being prepared in a peculiar way for the wider and more important tasks of his later years. Under the sheer stress of circumstances he then developed those qualities of persistence and pertinacity, amid seemingly insuperable difficulties, of resource and tact in negotiation, which have been so apparent on a wide canvas for all the world to see in more recent days. And from the early days until now, Dr. White has been "the splendid optimist." No one with a pessimistic outlook could have accomplished one tithe of what stands to his credit. With the eye of a prophet he has seen the vision, and he has pursued it with an unfaltering confidence in its sure fulfilment.

That Dr. White is a great ecclesiastical statesman all his countrymen are now agreed. But it is hoped in this record of his life to show another side to his character. The man has never been lost in the ecclesiastic. He may not " wear his heart upon his sleeve," yet he has a very human side to his personality. Strong man as he is, there is likewise a tender strain in his character. He is also a great deal more than a powerful figure in the Church Courts. With his deep religious convictions, true to the Evangelical traditions he has inherited, he is a preacher who declares the Gospel in all its fulness. In what follows it will be sought to show not only the course of this many-sided life, but also to trace some of the sources of its influence and the development of its power, as well as the wide range of its activities and influence.

CHAPTER II

ANCESTRY AND EARLY INFLUENCES

It has been said that while genius and great-ness are born and not inherited, the special qualities which in each case characterise them can usually be traced to some ancestor or ancestors, immediate or remote. In the case of Dr. White, at any rate, it is possible to trace in his ancestry the origin of influences which have not only largely shaped his career but have also to a great extent given him his supreme fitness for the special work in the ecclesiastical life of Scotland which Providence had in store for him.

Although he was born in the city of Glasgow, and in what was then part of the Barony Parish of which he is now minister, he may really be said to be a son of Ayrshire, the land of Burns. His forebears for several generations had their home in the parish of Kilwinning, where his father, Matthew White, was for many years a well-known grain merchant, miller and farmer. Matthew White, who was himself a native of Partick, made his home in Glasgow for a short period, and it was there his youngest son John was born on December 16, 1867, in what was

then the suburb of Sandyford. Shortly thereafter, however, the household returned to the
country, and it was with the small town of
Kilwinning, famous in history for its ancient
Abbey, the picturesque ruins of which are still
standing, and also notable for its early connec-
tions with Freemasonry and Archery in Scotland,
that the childhood and boyhood of John White
were associated.

Going back another generation, it can be seen
how rich and rare was the inheritance of the man
who was destined many years later to be the leader
of the movement for bringing the two great
Presbyterian Churches of Scotland into one.
Dr. White's grandfather on the maternal side,
James Kennedy, a farmer in the parish of Kilwinning, left the Church of Scotland at the
Disruption of 1843, and was one of the first elders
in Kilwinning Free Church. He was a man of
noted piety. It was often said, "There is no
need of a minister at a death-bed or a funeral
if we have James Kennedy." Carping criticism of ministers made in his presence was
never allowed to pass unchecked. Whatever
the denomination of the minister his invariable
reproof was, "You have no right to speak of a
servant of God in that way." Ecclesiastically
he was by no means exclusive, and he had little
sympathy with ecclesiastical prejudice. It is
related that on one occasion he interviewed a
prominent Free Church laird (to whom he was
personally unknown) about a farm which was

to let. After some discussion regarding terms, the laird remarked, " You have made a good offer, Mr. Kennedy, but I may tell you that I am thinking of giving the farm to another applicant who belongs to the Free Church." When he was informed that his visitor was an elder in the Free Church the atmosphere, which had up till that time been somewhat frigid, became much more genial. But this did not favourably impress James Kennedy. When he came home and told his wife of the interview, he shook his head sadly as he recalled the incident. Although his Church connection would have told in his favour, he was pained by the thought of such narrow-mindedness.

The wife of James Kennedy (Dr. White's grandmother) was described as " a woman of strong will and dignified demeanour." Her grandchildren stood more in awe of her than of their grandfather. For her, as for her husband, religion was a matter for daily life. It is related that during one season when the sowing or the reaping was delayed by the unfavourable weather her own faith never faltered and she always strengthened the faith of the household with the assurance : " We have been promised a seed time and a harvest." When nearing her end at the age of seventy, she said to her children, " I hope when my time comes I shall have the strong faith of your father "—and her prayer was answered.

Such were the parents of Marion Kennedy,

who became the wife of Matthew White and the mother of the subject of this biography. She was the eldest of the family and, like her mother, a woman of strong character. As became the daughter of a Free Church elder, she was one of the Sustentation Fund collectors in the congregation. Like her father, however, she was singularly free from ecclesiastical prejudice. When it became known that she was engaged to a member of the " Big Kirk," as it was called, a Free Church elder advised her to do her best, after her marriage, to bring her husband to the Free Church. The advice was refused, briefly but decisively. She went with her husband to the Parish Church, and to the end of her long life this strong Free Church woman found in the Church of Scotland a congenial and happy spiritual home. Blest with the best of health throughout all her many years, she was full of abounding activity and, indeed, never knew what it was to be idle. In her later years, when the cares of a family and of a household no longer occupied her time, she was a diligent worker for bazaars and other church efforts. Her interest in churches and ministers was proverbial, and it was maintained to the very end. Visitors were always welcome in her hospitable home, but none more so than ministers. For many years she delighted in Spurgeon's sermons, and in her later life she specially enjoyed the works of Dr. Alexander Smellie. As recently as 1920, this strong, gracious Scotswoman, then in her eighty eighth year, passed away in a full age " like as a shock of corn cometh in its season." She lived to witness many changes in the ecclesiastical life of Scotland and on these, through her children and her children's children, she had left her mark more deeply than she could ever have dreamed.

Matthew White, Dr. White's father, who died a comparatively young man in 1882 at the age of 51, was held in great esteem by all the workers in his employment. No strike or lock-out ever took place in any of his mills. He took a deep interest in all his employees, and impressed everyone by his high ideals of commercial integrity. Generally spoken of as a " brainy " man, he was noted for his foresight and for his milling engineering skill, and his advice was often sought in business matters. He had decided opinions, perhaps in advance of his time, about the standardisation of stipends, a fact which is of particular interest in view of the part taken by Dr. White in getting the standardising of ministers' stipends inserted in the Church of Scotland (Property and Endowments) Act, 1925. The Rev. William Lee Kerr, of Kilwinning, speaking at the induction dinner of the Rev. William White at Crosshouse in 1895 stated that the new minister's father, Mr. Matthew White, had often said to him that it was unreasonable that ministers' stipends should be ruled by the foreign market, and that some safer method should be employed of fixing the figures.

Matthew White, it is interesting to know, was

16

a great admirer of Dr. Norman Macleod, little dreaming that his own son was in after years to follow that great Scotsman in the pulpit of the Barony Church, Glasgow. He was a subscriber to *Good Words* from the very first, and his family remember well the delight with which they heard him reading aloud in the family circle portions of " The Old Lieutenant and his Son," and of " The Starling," and " Wee Davie." Though, like a patriotic Scot and an Ayrshire man, he was keen on Burns, it is recalled that Shakespeare was oftener in his hands. A Liberal in politics, he was an enthusiastic follower of W. E. Gladstone for many a day, but his faith in his hero was not so strong in his later years. It was somewhat unusual for this " pillar " of the Church of Scotland to be an adherent of Liberalism, and it was as strange that his father-in-law, the Free Church elder, should be a Conservative. This was really a reversal of the usual order and another indication of the strong, distinctive personality of these two representative figures.

Such were some of the forbears of Dr. White, and it is clear that the characteristics of his ancestry on both sides have contributed to his inheritance and helped to make him the man he is. Strength of character, " brainy " power, an indomitable will, deep religious conviction and broad-minded freedom from ecclesiastical prejudice—all these can be traced back to one or other of his ancestors in the generations that have gone before. And it is surely significant and striking that the son of a Church of Scotland member, who is also the grandson of a Free Church elder who "came out" at the Disruption of 1843, should be the leader in the movement for the reunion of the Church of Scotland and the United Free Church in 1929.

CHAPTER III

BOYHOOD AND SCHOOL DAYS

IN the home of his boyhood John White was reared in a district singularly rich in its historical associations, and it could not have been without effect on the mind and outlook of the boy that at an impressionable age he breathed such an atmosphere. Kilwinning, which is the traditional birthplace of Freemasonry in Scotland, was also famed for its Archery since 1488. Its July shooting at the popinjay on the steeple, 105 feet high, is described in Sir Walter Scott's "Old Mortality."

Yet, as the Rev. W. Lee Kerr said in his work on "Kilwinning Abbey," published in 1885: "Kilwinning is nothing if it is not ecclesiastical. It is true that Archers and Freemasons look to our district as one in which the twang of the bow and the tune of the 'Merry Masons' have resounded for centuries and that, too, with a frequency and a force seldom experienced elsewhere. But our fame rests on our ecclesiastical connection. Indeed, we live and move among names, and places, and stories, which remind us of nothing so much as the fact that we are what we are, because, 'in ages dim,' and in ages not dim, our parish has been associated with matters religious. Outside of our town we have the estates of Monkcastle and Monkridden, and a Druid's Grove—'our three-hilled altar by old Garnock's side'—and the well of St. Winning. Within the town we have the streets and lanes of Alms Wall and Abbey Gate, the Byres and the Green, Dove Cot Lane, the Cross Brae and the Corsehill, and we have strange stones peering out on one or two of our oldest buildings as if almost ashamed of their old-world faces, yet determined to speak to us of the distant past ; and in the walls that surround the town and the gables of our houses there are the strongest indications of our ancestors having made themselves comfortable at the expense of the magnificent Abbey, whose ruins still attest its ancient greatness, and the folk-lore, the fireside stories of Kilwinning, concern Monasteries and Monks and Steeples and Bells and St. Winning's Fairs."

The ancient Abbey, or at any rate part of it, was in use as the Parish Church until 1775, when a separate Church was built for parochial worship. In 1814 the remaining ruins of the monastery were greatly damaged by the fall of its fine, lofty tower. The tower was then rebuilt on a smaller scale to a height of 105 feet. At the same time considerable alterations were made in the choir of the Abbey Church and in parts of the nave.

When boys, John White and his brothers attended Kilwinning Parish Church, two miles distant from their home. He has, it may be mentioned at this point, three brothers still living. The two elder have followed their father as grain merchants and millers and are in business in Glasgow. The other brother is the Rev. William White, B.D., minister of Crosshouse, Kilmarnock, and Clerk of the Presbytery of Irvine.

There were two services every Sunday in summer, and one in winter, and also a Sunday School which was held in the hamlet of Dalgarven close at hand. Reasons or excuses for the non-attendance of children at church, which are regarded as valid by many parents to-day, had little or no weight with the parents of Dr. White. Illness was the only excuse which to their minds could justify any absence. And yet that household was no place of gloom on Sundays ; neither the drawn blinds nor the spirit of the drawn blinds had any place in their home. The children were not forbidden to take a walk on the Sunday afternoon. As a matter of fact their father sometimes accompanied them along the banks of the River Garnock past the mill dam and further on to the old mill dam in the direction of Dalry through scenery which, if not equal to " the banks and braes o' Bonnie Doon," of Burns poem, had yet a beauty of its own.

It was on the mill dam, not many yards from his father's mill, that John White learned the art of curling when he was a boy ; but the game which he and other boys of his time most enjoyed was a combination of skating and shinty. Needless to say the mill dam was useful, in summer, as a swimming pond.

The first seven years of John White's education were spent at the public school of Kilwinning. The headmaster, Mr. John Copeland, was a fine type of the old parochial schoolmaster. As an educationist he believed in giving a thorough grounding in the rudiments. John White and other boys who, after passing Standard VI were sent to Irvine Academy, found this to be of great advantage, and they and their school were often complimented by the English master of the Academy.

One of the teachers on the staff, Mr. Harwood, who had conducted a private school before School Boards came into existence, did not possess all the qualifications of some of the younger men, but he had one special gift which meant a great deal for some of his pupils—he was a splendid teacher of the Bible lesson. Another of the teachers was Mr. James F. Arthur, who has been for many years one of the Lecturers in the Bible Training Institute, Glasgow. While he was able, without any apparent effort, to maintain excellent discipline and keep his pupils at their work, Mr. Arthur at the same time gained their admiration. He had been a member of a famous Glasgow football team, and occasionally he joined the boys in the playground and took part in their game of football. Such a thing was less common then than it is to-day, and it made the schoolboys proud of their teacher.

BOYHOOD AND SCHOOL DAYS

Unlike the case of some men who have risen to fame, it was not late in life before John White's abilities blossomed forth. He was a promising scholar from the very first, and at the public school he was one of the regular prize winners. And, even when still a school boy, he proved that he had " all his wits about him." One Wednesday his father, on returning from the weekly visit to the Glasgow Grain Market, brought home a telephone. This gave the boys what was in those days a wonderful experience, for, standing a hundred yards away from their father, they could hear his voice distinctly over the wire. John, not yet in his teens, was allowed to take the instrument to the school with him next day, so that his fellow scholars might see and hear the novelty for themselves. As the telephone was being demonstrated in the playground the head master came along. Becoming interested in it himself, Mr. Copeland told John White to go to the other end and speak to him in order that he might test the apparatus. John did as he was told and the message he sent over the wire to the headmaster was: " Mr. Copeland, will you please give us sixpence for our football club?" Needless to say the request was granted. This was Dr. White's first appeal for a collection. It was also the first known example of his readiness to seize an opportunity and, in this case, the boy was father of the man.

From Kilwinning Public School John White proceeded, as did other "lads o' pairts," to

Irvine Royal Academy. At Irvine he was daily within sight and sound of the sea. The view from the ancient town, as a local historian has described it, was one to be remembered. Looking out over the sandhills and the belt of blue in the Firth of Clyde, there rose the peaks of Arran which evening by evening were bathed in splendour as the sun sank slowly in the rear. Up the river Garnock and across the breezy moor the level was bounded by the Eglinton woods, while on the other side the fields through which the Irvine flows led upwards to the heights of Dundonald. The outlook was not marred but, in the eyes of some, rather made more picturesque, by the sight of the iron works at Kilwinning and Ardeer, and the furnace fires which gleamed out on the western horizon, blending not inharmoniously with the colours of the sky at dawn.

Irvine is one of the old historic towns of Scotland, with a Charter dating from the twelfth century. It was the seat of one of the oldest Presbyteries in Scotland, having been erected in 1581, the same year which saw the erection of Glasgow and of Edinburgh as the first of the Scottish Presbyteries. It was famous also as one of the centres of influence in the years of active evangelical effort which followed the Reformation. Three of Scotland's hymn writers were associated with Irvine—James Montgomery who wrote " Hail to the Lord's Anointed," David Dickson, author of " O

Mother, dear Jerusalem," and Mrs. Cousin, the "Scottish Christina Rossetti," whose hymn "The Sands of Time are Sinking" is sung in all the churches. Irvine was also the scene of the life-work of W. B. Robertson, the poet-preacher of the United Presbyterian Church, while John Galt, the author of that Scottish classic, "The Annals of the Parish," was a native of the town, and the local colour can be traced in most of his books.

In order to be in Irvine in time for the opening hour at the Academy John White had to leave his home every morning at 7.30 and it was 5.30 in the afternoon before he returned. Then two hours had to be devoted to home lessons, which meant altogether a long day for a boy of thirteen years of age. At the Academy, however, he was again fortunate in his teachers. The English master, Mr. Peter Monie, was an efficient teacher, and his lessons in Bible knowledge were a feature of his work. Mr. Monie was proud of the success of his former pupils, and on his retirement in 1914, after thirty-seven years' service, he secured Dr. White, as the minister of the Barony, and one of the most distinguished "old boys" of the Academy, to present the prizes and make the valedictory speech.

The teacher for Latin and Greek was the Rev. R. B. Pattie, B.D., a graduate of Glasgow University, who gained the Black Theological Fellowship while teaching at Irvine. He was held in very high esteem by his pupils for his lovable nature and his deep interest in their work, and they responded to his influence.

Irvine Academy had a distinguished roll of pupils, especially in regard to the Civil Service. But it is worthy of note that since the beginning of the present century it has sent forth four Moderators of the Scottish Churches. Dr. James Curdie Russell of Campbeltown, whose patriarchal figure is so well remembered, was Moderator of the Church of Scotland General Assembly in 1902, and Dr. Robert Howie of Govan was Moderator of the United Free Church General Assembly in the same year. Dr. John Brown of Bellahouston was Moderator of the Church of Scotland General Assembly in 1916, and Dr. John White in 1925.

Two years were spent by John White at Irvine Royal Academy, where he repeated his successes at Kilwinning as a prizeman, and gave further promise of a great future before he left to pursue his studies at the University of Glasgow.

CHAPTER IV

THE STUDENT IN ARTS

When John White entered the University of Glasgow as a student he did so with certain distinct personal advantages. It has always been the case that many students at the Scottish Universities have found it necessary to use part of their time in some form of work by which they could supplement the family income until they were able to complete their course. John White was under no such necessity. His father's circumstances were such as to make it possible for him to give his undivided time and attention to his studies and to the life of the University generally. This independence as to ways and means did not, however, lead to any slackening of his own efforts. Work was congenial to him then as it has been throughout all his career. He threw himself wholeheartedly into his studies and also into the varied activities of the students' societies.

In his Arts course he took from the very first a leading place, and, among a band of distinguished students, his pre-eminence was soon acknowledged. One of his contemporaries, the

DR. JOHN WHITE

Rev. Professor Ernest F. Scott, D.D., of the Union Theological Seminary, New York, writes :

" I was contemporary with John White at Glasgow University in the late eighties, under a very remarkable group of teachers. Kelvin, Jebb, Edward Caird were admittedly the first living authorities on their several subjects. Nichol, Jack, Ramsay, Veitch were all outstanding men— rare personalities as well as great scholars. The University was in many ways sadly backward according to modern standards, but it is comforting to reflect that there are some things which do not necessarily go with improved equipment and organisation. We had the most brilliant staff which ever served a University, and we had also an extraordinary number of able men among the students. Many of them came up without much previous training, and would now be refused admission ; but some of the best men were made out of this unpromising material. We were all trained in five or six set subjects, by methods which had not greatly changed since the Middle Ages, but the new system of education will do well if it can show equal results after thirty or forty years.

" I knew John White almost from the day he entered college, but we never, so far as I can remember, took a class together. The reason was that although he came up fresh from school he turned at once to the philosophical course, which most of us left over till our closing years. He was the youngest member of the Logic class, which then numbered several hundreds, and he astonished every one by coming out first prizeman. This made us all regard him as something of an infant phenomenon, but he soon showed that he was as different as possible from the unhealthy type of youth who has developed one special aptitude by hot-house processes, and stops his growth when other minds are just beginning. Although he preserved and matured his philosopical gift his interests were always expanding. In his later University years he was editor of the Magazine, chief orator at the Union, organiser of his party at the Rectorial election, acknowledged leader in almost all the college activities. Coming as he did in the great period of transition in Scottish University life his influence was in many respects decisive.

" My more intimate acquaintance with him was largely through James Gemmill, who afterwards became professor of biology at Dundee. Gemmill had one of the finest minds I have ever known. After his Arts course he went in for medicine, and in spite of constant ill-health did notable original work in biological science. But he could have distinguished himself equally in philosophy, in literature, in almost any branch of learning. If he were still living he could have written a better appreciation of John White than any of his contemporaries. To all appearance they were very different. Gemmill was quiet and meditative, White abounded in energy and was expansive and eloquent. But at bottom they were kindred souls and drew naturally together. Perhaps the most valuable part of my college education was my intercourse with those two men, especially when we went down together for short vacations to Gemmill's home at Mauchline—the farm just adjoining Mossgiel. I at least shared the taste for tobacco with the other two, and took part, to that extent, in wonderful discussions, sometimes only broken off at dawn. What they were all about I cannot now recall, but I have no doubt that much of my thinking since would be found to go back to them. One thing that will always remain is the memory of those two gifted minds, both so fresh and earnest, seeking together for some clearer light on the mystery of things."

Of two of the famous Professors under whom he studied in his Arts course Dr. White himself has given striking appreciations. On the occasion of the Kelvin Centenary he made a speech at the meeting of Glasgow Presbytery on June 26th, 1924, when he paid a tribute to his former teacher which, because of the light it throws on his personal impressions, may be quoted in full. He said :

" To-morrow is the centenary of the birth of William Thomson, Lord Kelvin, one of the greatest men of science of our own and every age, and one of the humblest and devoutest Christians : it is fitting that we should make record of the event in the minutes of our Presbytery.

" Many members of this Presbytery were students of his class, and, whether we learned much or little of experimental science, we sat in wonderment at his vast knowledge of every branch of physical science, and above all we learned to reverence and to love him as one of God's great gifts to the world, whose heart was as big as his brain.

" Born in Belfast one hundred years ago, he came to live within a stone's cast of this Presbytery House at the age of eight : at the age of ten years he entered the University ; seven years later he was in Cambridge, and at the age of twenty-two he was Professor of Natural Philosophy in Glasgow University.

" I leave it to others more qualified to pass eulogy on the man of science, the greatest physicist of our own time and one of the most illustrious of all ages. Some of us have a vague memory of his lectures, or broken conversations going off every moment at a tangent, on thermo dynamics, the principle of the dissipation of energy, the mysteries of electricity and magnetism, of cables and compasses; and as he opened up wondrous worlds to us we felt how abysmal was our ignorance, and I fear had to leave it at that.

" Some deep impressions remain. No one will ever forget the lessons taught us by coming into contact with this great personality, so zealous, so modest, so patient in toil, so inflexible in faith—the lessons of humility and of deepest reverence for the Creator of all things. To us he was a man of giant intellect which was only equalled by his greater diffidence. He was always and untiringly seeking, as if his human energy knew no dissipation, to discover the deepest secrets of God's ocean, earth and sky. His every discovery, and his original findings, which were numerous, only deepened his veneration and his theism. From him we learned that science, when religious, as all true science is, humbled the heart and bowed the knee. Science falsely so called had no place in his equipment to dim his vision of God and of God's world. He exemplified the saying of Goethe that man was not made to solve the problem of existence ; he was made to attempt it, that he might know the limits of the unknowable.

" The great Newton, a short time before his death, said : ' I do not know what I may appear to the world, but to myself I seem to have been only like a little boy playing on the sea-shore and diverting myself now and then finding a smoother pebble or a prettier shell than ordinary, while the great ocean of truth lay all undiscovered before me.'

" Many will remember the touching and modest confession of Kelvin at the time of his jubilee as a professor, when men of highest distinction in all walks of life assembled in Glasgow to pay tribute to his genius, that after having spent fifty years in the endeavour to discover the ultimate meaning even of the primitive constituents of matter he was obliged to confess that he had failed, and that the mystery was as great as ever. ' We know in part,' was the confession of his intellect ; the confession of his faith knew no incompleteness.

" I would move that on the occasion of the centenary of the birth of this great sage, who will remain for all time one of the chief distinctions of our city, we place on record our gratitude to God for His gift to the world in this man of great genius and invincible faith."

But the great influence over John White when he was an Arts student at Glasgow University was undoubtedly that of Professor Edward Caird, who then occupied the Chair of Moral Philosophy and afterwards went to Oxford as Master of Balliol. A memorial article attracted the attention of Mrs. Caird and brought from her a letter of warm appreciation. " The article," she wrote, " characterised my dear husband with such completeness of understanding that I prized it as one of the most valuable, and expressed with a simple beauty and clearness that made it perfect. I saw it was written by a former student and begged of my sister-in-law to give me the clue. . . . Only to-day I have heard that you are the writer. You have given me deep pleasure, not only for your strong personal testimony, but for the belief that it may acquaint some who read it, who had no other channel, with what his teaching and his life were."

In the course of the article, Dr. White gives these personal impressions of the teacher who influenced him so profoundly :

" A spiritual atmosphere pervaded Edward

Caird's class-room ; and in the presence of the
threatening forces of materialism, men were
taught to interpret the world and life in spiritual
terms.   When one thinks of the many brilliant
students Caird sent forth to teach others—half
the philosophical chairs in the country and several
beyond the seas are occupied by them—and how
all are imbued with and loyal to his lofty idealism,
it is hardly too much to say that Caird saved his
age from materialism.   His influence on theology
is acknowledged on all sides, and it has been
said that the clergy, or rather the congregations,
owe much to him.   Some thirty years ago he was
accounted heretical by the orthodox ; but thirty
years are a long time in the theological thinking
of Scotland, and the orthodox of to-day would
have been heretical then.   There was nothing
of the dogmatic theologian about him ; there
was nothing of the agnostic.   He held that it
was possible to maintain a critical spirit without
agnosticism and a reasonable faith without dogmat-
ism.   He had a devout reverence for Christ
and His teachings ; Christianity was the abso-
lute religion.   The one thing necessary was not
dogmatic correctness, but devotion to the cause
of God and humanity, and ' however important it
is that our thoughts about God, about Christ,
about the relations of God to man, and of man
to God, should be as adequate as we can make
them, yet the root of the matter lies in the spirit
of Christ, and not in doctrines about Him; in
the living realisation of the nearness of the finite

life to the infinite, and not in the theological exactness of our creed.' Caird never imposed his views on any one ; he urged men to think for themselves, and not to move intellectually in great masses, led by a few who thought and spoke for all. A chief note in all his teaching was faith in the wisdom and goodness of the divine power which orders our lives. His last published word was a lay sermon on the faith of Job—' Though He slay me, yet will I trust Him.' All's well with the world, for the world is divinely ordered, and the injustices and sufferings that are inexplicable now will ultimately be fully justified. In speaking on immortality to his Oxford students he said— was he thinking of the life-companionship with his famous brother ?—' every one who has known intimately a great and good man, feels death in his case to be almost incredible, if by death be meant an end of being. If the world is rational, and therefore a moral system, it cannot be that this, the most precious thing we know, the only absolutely precious thing in the world, a character built up and matured in goodness through all the trials of life, should pass away and be lost for ever.' Edward Caird is to many of us another proof of immortality, for his was undoubtedly a character built up and matured in goodness. He and his work remain. His teaching was valuable because it was so generative, and introduced the young mind to the ' grand thoughts that never can be wearied out.' "

Among the contemporaries of Dr. White as a

student in Arts, in addition to Professor Ernest F. Scott (whose impressions have been quoted), were the Right Hon. Sir Robert Horne, M.P., and not a few others whose names afterwards became widely known. Up till this time Dr. White had been pursuing his University course with the view of entering the legal profession. This was not at all surprising to those who were associated with him. His whole bent seemed to lie in that direction. His clear logical mind, his strong common sense, his gifts of speech and his dexterity as a debater marked him out as one sure to shine in the legal world. John White and Robert Horne were the two on whom the hopes of their fellow students were mainly centred. And when it became known that John White had decided to turn from Law to Divinity, the common remark among their contemporaries was that the path to the Lord Chancellorship had been cleared for Robert Horne !

A fellow student writing of this period says—" We all realized that John White was a man who would step into the first place whatever line of life he chose. Had he gone in for Law he would have risen to be Lord Chancellor, and had he gone into the Church of England he would have become an Archbishop."

CHAPTER V

FROM LAW TO DIVINITY

WHAT, it may be asked, was responsible for turning John White from Law to Divinity ? It is not, however, altogether easy to answer this question. There was in his case no dramatic decision taken under the stress of some great crisis in his life. The " change over " came as the result of influences which had been quietly at work in his mind and heart over a considerable period before they actually blossomed into fruit.

What these influences were it may never be possible fully to know, but some of them, at least, can be definitely traced. There was, in the first place, as already indicated, the inheritance he received at his birth from more than one generation of his ancestors. Then there was the home influence in which he was reared, than which there was no stronger influence in his life. From homes such as that of his parents it is true, in the words of Burns, that " old Scotia's grandeur springs " but it is equally true that in such homes there has also been the secret of the splendid succession of the Scottish pulpit. It was a home where religion was a reality ; where the Church was given its true place, and where the pulpit, unconsciously as well as by direct inference, loomed before the children as one of the greatest spheres in life. The fact that two members of that family circle dedicated themselves to the ministry is in itself a proof of the strong and deep influence which pervaded the household.

It cannot be said that Dr. White was greatly influenced by any of the Church of Scotland ministers of his youth. He seemed rather to be groping for something he failed to find. During his University days, however, he frequently went to hear Dr. John Hunter in Trinity Congregational Church. Hunter was then at the very beginning of what became a powerful ministry, attracting in particular the thoughtful youth of all classes. He was, after Dr. John Caird, as Principal Story once remarked at a public dinner, "the students' preacher." It was not because he met all his difficulties, or solved all his problems, or was his perfect ideal, that John White was attracted by John Hunter. But he found in him a preacher who, at least, was facing up to some of the things with which he himself was battling. And so, on many a Sunday, he made his way to Trinity Church to join the cosmopolitan crowd clamouring for admission to its services.

Two other Glasgow ministers attracted him for different reasons. One was the Rev. G. L. Carstairs of Berkeley Street United Presbyterian Church, a persuasive evangelical preacher, and the other the Rev. F. H. Robarts of Hillhead Baptist Church, a man of saintly and gracious personality.

In both of these the young student found something which satisfied him at that period in his life, and thus these two honoured ministers, although they little knew it, were contributing to the development of one who in later days was to influence so profoundly the whole Church life of Scotland.

Perhaps, however, the main influence that sent John White into the ministry, as he himself would acknowledge, was the teaching of Professor Edward Caird in Moral Philosophy. In his tribute to Edward Caird already quoted he said that " Caird never impressed his views on anyone ; he urged men to think for themselves." In that last sentence there lies, perhaps, a large part of the secret of John White's decision to leave the study of law for the study of divinity, and to devote his life to the ministry. In thinking for himself as Edward Caird had taught him, he found there was something behind the last word in philosophy, and that there were problems and needs which nothing human could ever meet and satisfy. He fought his own intellectual battles until in the end he came to the sure foundation of faith on which his subsequent life has been built.

But even after he had decided to study for the ministry his course was for a time uncertain. Reference has already been made to his attendance at Trinity Congregational Church and Berkeley Street United Presbyterian Church. When he definitely decided to devote his life to the ministry, influences were at work seeking to draw him to

Congregationalism with inducements in the way of a special theological training in England. Then there was the pull of the United Presbyterian Church, into whose Theological Hall at Edinburgh there had gone some of his most brilliant contemporaries at Glasgow University. Eventually, however, he took what was, after all, the natural course, and followed his elder brother in entering the Divinity Hall of Glasgow University to prepare for the ministry of the Church of Scotland in which he had been reared.

It was in 1889 that John White began his Divinity course at the University of Glasgow. There were four Professors under whom he studied. In the Chair of Divinity was Professor William Purdie Dickson, who had been promoted to that position from the Chair of Biblical Criticism when Dr. John Caird became Principal of the University. His succession to so eminent a teacher was said to have " strong justification on grounds of scholarship and awareness of contemporary theological movements," and his students were unanimous in their testimony to his " fatherly and friendly supervision." From Caird himself came the significant testimony that " his heart was as warm as his head was clear."

The Chair of Church History was occupied by Professor R. H. Story, who afterwards became Principal of the University, and Principal Clerk and Moderator of the General Assembly of the Church of Scotland. His picturesque personality, power of pungent speech, and strength of character made perhaps a stronger impression on the students even than his lectures, characteristically brilliant as they were. There was much in him that appealed to John White. The younger man did not always follow the counsels of the elder (as will be shown later on) but he felt the power of his personality and, in spite of all the differences between them, there grew up between the two a mutual feeling of warm appreciation.

Of Dr. Story as a Professor, Dr. White has written : " As a student in his class of Church History I can speak of the passionate love for the National Church, and the enthusiastic devotion to its further development and extension, that characterised his brilliant lectures. I can recall the lectures, marked by fine sympathetic insight and impartiality, in which he graphically pictured the life and work of John Knox, ' the grandest figure in the entire history of the British Reformation ' ; and how, with incisive speech, he upheld the universal priesthood of believers, the spiritual independence of the Church of Christ, the validity of the Orders of the Church of Scotland, the rights and privileges of the Scottish people in their National Church, the necessity of the liberty of the spirit to the healthy growth and development of the Church, and the authority of the Bible (especially the Gospel) as the Rule of Faith."

Dr. White has also defended Dr. Story against some personal misapprehensions. " To those who sat under him," he says, "the frequent description of Dr. Story as cold and distant is, while not inexplicable, yet most inaccurate. His students, whom he inspired with a deep loyalty to the Church, admired his cultured scholarship, his breadth of view, his hatred of cant, and his direct speech that paid first regard to truth and none to consequence ; and knowing him in the privacy of his hospitable home, they were not only proud of him, but loved him as one of the most generous and tender-hearted of men. With many others I can speak of the continued interest he took in his students when they had left the class-room to enter upon the duties of the ministry, and how he was ever ready in the hour of difficulty to give the word of counsel and encouragement."

Professor Stewart of the Chair of Biblical Criticism, and Professor Robertson of the Chair of Hebrew, seem to have made no particular impression on John White, although in Biblical Criticism, as in Divinity and Church History, he was first prizeman. Hebrew did not appeal to him and he did not throw himself whole-heartedly into its study. Years afterwards Professor Robertson, in referring to his work in the Hebrew Class, said of John White that "he did not come to the help of the Lord, to the help of the Lord against the mighty" but he was quite sure that if he had only taken up the subject of Hebrew he would have excelled in it as he did in all his other classes.

One day in Professor Stewart's class-room John White was busy correcting the proofs of the University Magazine of which he was the editor, while the class went on with its study of New Testament Greek. The Professor, evidently suspicious, pounced upon White with the request that he would translate the next passage. A friend passed along the Greek Testament, pointing out the place, and White rose and, without any sign of hesitation, at once translated the passage correctly as if his whole attention had been concentrated on the lesson.

"Very good," remarked the Professor. "And now Mr. Joannes White will you give me your opinion as to what that passage shows?" the passage being that in the Gospel of St. Mark relating the case of the woman who had suffered many things at the hands of many physicians. "It shows," replied White, "what may be called the humour of the Evangelist." "Humour of the Evangelist!" exclaimed the Professor. "I never heard of such a thing." Professor Stewart, it may be explained, had a pet theory that St. Luke's Gospel was written before St. Mark's and when White began by saying that the passage confirmed the view that Mark had written after Luke, the class applauded noisily. Then White went on to say that when Mark used the words of Luke, the physician, in describing the woman as having suffered many things of many physicians, his humour was shown by the added touch of his own that "she was nothing bettered but rather the worse." At this clever and palpable hit the class again applauded vehemently. For the moment the Professor was speechless and then, as if anxious to drop the subject quickly, he pointed to another student with the remark, " Will Mr. —— carry on ? "

A fellow student has said that John White at the Divinity Hall stepped into the first place right away and impressed all of them with his outstanding personality. Even then he revealed his qualities as a leader of men, and one example of this may be cited. In the last year of his course he got all the Divinity students together and put before them a practical proposition. " We have been listening," he said, " to lectures on all sorts of theological subjects, but we have got little practical guidance as to how we are to conduct ourselves in our parishes. For instance, what about our relationship with heritors and about the general work of the parish ? " He urged that some guidance should be given on these and other practical affairs. His fellow students all agreed with him and he was deputed, along with Mr. A. B. Scott, (now minister of Helmsdale) to see Professor Story with the object of securing some lectures of the kind. Dr. Story fell in with the suggestion, but there was, later on, a more important development when it was decided to institute a course of Lectures on Pastoral Theology in the Divinity Halls of all the four Scottish Universities. To Dr. White's action in his student days may be attributed the origin of this most valuable feature of the theological curriculum.

Dr. Story's lectures on this particular subject were characteristic of the man and symptomatic of the age in which they were delivered. Happily few, if any, of the students—and Dr. White least of all—fell under his influence in regard to the relations which he suggested should be observed with other Churches. The ecclesiastical atmosphere then was very different from what it is to-day. Disestablishment was a great battle cry, and fighting speeches were being delivered in the United Presbyterian Church by that stalwart of the cause, Dr. George C. Hutton of Paisley, while in the Free Church Principal Rainy was also in his own way an advocate of the policy. Dr. Story, on the other hand, was uncompromising in the attitude he adopted and in the advice he gave to his students. He counselled them, when they became parish ministers, to have as little to do with the ministers of the dissenting Churches as possible, and on no account to exchange pulpits with them even although they wished to do so. " No doubt," he said, " they are brethren, but gentlemen, treat them always as " erring brethren." All this is a curious commentary on the change of attitude and the happier relations now existing. Had Dr. White followed the advice of his teacher in this matter there might have been a different story to tell to-day of the history of the Church in Scotland.

The place taken by John White as a student can best be indicated by the following list of his University record :

DR. JOHN WHITE

First-Class Certificate in Latin.

First-Class Certificate in Greek.

First-Class Certificate in English Literature.

First Prize in Logic Class—Special work.

First Prize in Logic Class—Class work.

First Prize in Advanced Logic Class—Higher Metaphysics.

First Prize in Moral Philosophy—Class work.

First-Class Certificate in Higher Moral Philosophy Class.

First Prize in Political Economy—Essays.

First Prize in Political Economy—Class work.

First Prize Divinity—Essay.

Second Prize Divinity—Class work.

First Prize Divinity—Class work.

Third Prize Divinity—Class work.

First Prize Biblical Criticism—Essays.

Second Prize Biblical Criticism—Class work.

First Prize in Church History—Junior.

First Prize in Church History—Senior.

Bracketed first for the Class of Medical Jurisprudence.

Student in Zoology.

Student in Civil Law.

Ewing Gold Medal for best Essay on " France in 1789."

Gartmore Gold Medal for best Essay on " Democracy—Ancient and Modern."

Henderson Prize of Twenty Guineas for the best Essay on " Pre-Christian Institutions analogous to the Sabbath."

Coulter Prize—University Prize—for the best
  Essay on " Locke and Leibnitz."
Numerous Bursaries.
Graduated M.A. with Honours in Philosophy.

It became a legend in student circles that John
White might have had a First-Class in Philosophy
had he expounded the Hamiltonian philosophy
instead of condemning it—in other words been
more expository and less polemical.

The prominent part taken by John White in
connection with the various students' societies
at the University is still recalled by his associates.
He was the foremost figure of his time in under-
graduate circles, and held almost every office to
which he could be elected. The list of his
appointments is a lengthy one—President of the
Philomathic Society, President of the Philosophical Society, President of the Independent
Club, President of the Rectorial Club, President
of the Theological Society, Vice-President of the
Missionary Society, President of the Students'
Representative Council and Chief Editor of the
" Glasgow University Magazine." There are
those who still recall what they describe as " the
joyous irresponsibility with which he ran the
Independent Club," and the manner in which
he re-organised the Editorship of the University
Magazine. As a speaker and as an organiser
he was unsurpassed among the students of his
time, and his fellows turned to him instinctively
as the leader in all their activities.

Thirty years afterwards, when he became Moderator of the General Assembly, he was entertained at dinner by his former fellow students who presented him with a platinum chain and cross and an address of congratulation enriched with illustrations of the leading scenes of his life work. It was in the following terms :

" Right Reverend and Right Honourable,
" Your fellow students in the Divinity Hall of Glasgow University have learned with great gratification of your elevation to the Moderatorial Chair of the General Assembly, and they hereby unite in subscribing to an expression of deep satisfaction that one from among themselves should by his devotion to the work of the Church of Scotland, alike in parochial, presbyterial and national spheres, have won the confidence of all parties within the Church, and earned for himself the high honour which has now been conferred upon you by its General Assembly.

" We cordially congratulate you and pray Almighty God that He would grant you strength to carry through the onerous duties which will fall to your discharge and that His blessing may be upon you in all your ways."

The address was signed by seventy-five former fellow students now in the ministry of the Church throughout the land—a striking example of how the friendships of early days had survived the passing of many years.

When he completed his course his teachers testified in no uncertain terms to the impression he had made on them. Some of them were indeed prophetic and it may therefore be interesting to give the following extracts :

Principal Caird : " Mr. White was during his whole career a very distinguished student. He took first prizes in the Philosophy classes, and in almost all the classes in the Faculty of Divinity. . . . A man of excellent ability and culture. . . ."

Principal Story : " I never had a better student than Mr. White. . . . He always showed his possession of a clear and powerful mind and a large store of knowledge well digested of general culture and practical efficiency in method."

Professor Edward Caird (Master of Balliol) : " Mr. White was one of the most distinguished students of his time in the University of Glasgow, particularly in the departments of Philosophy and Theology. . . . In all his classes he showed himself to be one of the ablest and most diligent of the students. His work showed proof of an insight into the real bearing of philosophical questions which is by no means common. He is a man of character and energy, and had great influence among his fellow-students."

Professor Bradley : " From my knowledge of Mr. White I readily understood the high opinion formed of him by my colleagues in the Philosophical department, and the prominent place which he held among the students. There can be no doubt that he is a man whose intellectual power and force of character would make themselves speedily felt in whatever position he might occupy."

John White's first appointment in the Church was as assistant to Dr. J. W. King in the parish of New Kilpatrick, just outside Glasgow, and he was licensed by the Presbytery of Dumbarton on May 3rd, 1892. As part of his duties he acted as missionary at Drumchapel within the bounds of the parish, and a story is told in connection with his work there which illustrates how, even at that stage in his career, he would remain cool and unperturbed in face of circumstances which would upset most men, and particularly young men trying their 'prentice hand in the ministry.

On the way to the Mission Hall where the service was held, it was learned one Sunday that the leader of the praise had become suddenly ill and would be unable to be present. The hall was crowded. The young assistant announced the opening Psalm and, having explained the absence of the usual precentor, he asked if someone would "raise the tune." There was no response. After asking again and waiting for a minute or two, he suddenly began himself, only to discover that the tune he had started did not suit the metre of the verse. He did not stop but began the second line with another tune, and with no greater success. Even then he did not give up but continued in the third line singing a kind of mixture of the first two, while the fourth line, as he has said himself in commenting on the incident afterwards, " was quite original." All the while voices were occasionally chiming in to help in this valiant effort, but naturally with no great success. At the end of the verse White remarked, " We shall sing the Old Hundredth, and if we can't sing that we will have no singing to-night." Then the whole congregation rose to the occasion, and the singing is said to have been better than usual.

This incident was ample confirmation of an opinion once expressed by his mother—" If it were ever possible for John to break down in the pulpit, he would just bob up again."

In less than a year John White left the assistant-ship at New Kilpatrick to become minister of the parish of Shettleston, where he was very soon to begin to make history.

CHAPTER VI

SHETTLESTON

On March 14th, 1893, Mr. White was ordained to his first charge as minister of the parish of Shettleston and, in view of the stirring and memorable events of a few years later, and for a better understanding of their significance, it is necessary to trace briefly the story of the Church and parish.

At Shettleston, it has been said, we are on historic ground. Its place name is ancient. It appears in a charter of Alexander II, dated October 29th, 1226, wherein the Bailies of Rutherglen are prohibited from taking toll or custom " in the town of Glasgow, but at the Cross of Schedenestoun as they were anciently accustomed to be taken."

Shettleston also appears frequently, but under many orthographic variations, in the old rental books of the Barony of Glasgow. In 1912, under Glasgow's great annexation scheme, Shettleston was included within the bounds of the city of which it is now both a municipal and a Parliamentary division.

Turning to the ecclesiastical position we find that Shettleston was originally a part of the Barony Parish. Towards the middle of the eighteenth century, however, many of the inhabitants of the Eastern district of the Barony Parish, and of those residing in the Western and contiguous district of Old Monkland Parish, felt themselves " disadvantageously situated," with respect to " the means of grace," by reason of the distance they had to travel to their respective Parish Churches. It was also asserted that the disagreeable and almost impassable state of the roads during the winter season, and the vast extent of the parishes, rendered it impossible for their ministers to give them anything like an adequate amount of pastoral superintendence and instruction. They resolved, therefore, on having a place of worship erected in their own immediate locality.

The Rev. Laurence Hill, of the Barony, and his kirk session, gave their cordial consent to the Shettleston people to proceed. A site was granted by Messrs. James and George Reston, the joint proprietors of Budhill, on condition that a pew in the Church and a lair in the burying ground were reserved for them. The Church was erected entirely by private subscription, and it was opened in 1752.

It was the intention of the subscribers to secure the entire disjunction of the district of Shettleston, and its formation into a separate parish, but from legal and other causes this was at the time found to be impossible. The Church was used as a " preaching station " until 1788, when the Presbytery constituted it a Chapel of Ease, the Rev. Henry Musket, who was then in charge of the congregation, becoming the first ordained minister. But it was many years later before the dream of a separate parish could be realised.

In 1844, however, an Act was passed to facilitate the disjoining or dividing of extensive or populous parishes and the erection of new parishes. Shettleston, being within the Barony Parish, which, with a population of 120,000 persons, was within the scope of the Act, then had its opportunity, and it immediately took advantage of the new legislation. The result was that in 1847 it was "decerned and ordained that the district of Shettleston should be disjoined and erected into a new and distinct parish, and that the inhabitants of the district should repair to the Church of Shettleston as their proper Parish Church for hearing the Word of God, receiving the sacraments, and partaking in all other public acts of divine worship, and subject themselves to the Minister of the said Church and Parish of Shettleston as proper Parishioners thereof in all time coming."

On the second day of February, 1848, a copy of the decree of disjunction and erection was laid before the Presbytery of Glasgow, and the Rev. J. Macritchie Leckie took his seat in the Court as the first minister of the Parish. Mr. Leckie, who died in 1861, was succeeded by the Rev. Mathew Rodger who, three years later, became minister of St. Leonards, St. Andrews. Then came the long ministry of twenty-eight years—

Photo : Lafayette]

[Glasgow

SHETTLESTON PARISH CHURCH

from 1864 to 1892—of the Rev. Gilbert Johnston, one of whose daughters became the wife of the Very Rev. Dr. John Smith of Partick, who was Moderator of the General Assembly in 1922. It was on the death of Mr. Johnston that Mr. White was elected to Shettleston—for which there had been a strong leet of candidates—and his ordination took place there, as already stated, on March 14th, 1893.

It was not long before the striking personality and outstanding ability of the young minister made an impression. The people flocked to the Church until the pews became uncomfortably crowded, every inch of accommodation, even to the steps of the pulpit stairs, being fully occupied. The conditions soon became not only unpleasant but insanitary. The Church, then almost a century and a half old, was of a primitive design and faulty construction, and it was becoming much dilapidated. Some of the walls were bulging, others were torn with rents, and the roof was sagging. The only heating was from a stove, and as there was no proper ventilation, the decaying woodwork and damp walls and floor gave forth an unpleasant smell. When the Church became crowded, as it did from the outset of Mr. White's ministry, matters came to a crisis, as it was a common occurrence for two or three people, overcome by the atmosphere, to be carried out from almost every service.

Mr. White, young, enthusiastic and energetic, at once grasped the situation. He saw that

until a new church was built the work of the
congregation would be severely handicapped,
while any further development would be a practical impossibility. The need was obvious and
urgent ; to delay taking action would be to
sacrifice the best interests of the parish. In
view of all that happened later on it is necessary
that this should be made clear.

At this stage, and for the purpose of enabling
a fair estimate to be taken of the subsequent
proceedings, it would also be well to explain the
position in which the minister of Shettleston
found himself and the means he took to avoid any
trouble. According to the law as it then stood
the heritors of the Parish were responsible for
the cost of a new church. Mr. White resolved,
however, from the outset that every endeavour
should be made to secure the consent and co-operation of all parties concerned. His first step was
to discuss the situation with his office-bearers,
and he suggested that, before any approach was
made to the heritors, the congregation should
be asked to subscribe according to their ability.
As the result of a statement and appeal issued to
the members a substantial sum was raised in a
short time.

Thus fortified by the practical support of the
congregation, Mr. White approached the leading
heritors and he found them willing to contribute
towards the cost of the Church, which it was
estimated would be about £12,000 or £13,000.
A provisional agreement was duly signed by

these leading heritors and by Mr. White on behalf of the congregation. So far, all had gone well. According to law, however, this agreement had to be submitted to the whole of the heritors in the parish, including the real rent heritors and the small feuars. Political feeling at the moment ran high and when the meeting was held the smaller heritors, although it meant so little to them, outvoted the larger heritors on whom the main burden would have fallen. As this vote was final, matters came to a deadlock and the " Shettleston Case " attracted attention all over the country.

Although Mr. White had been so anxious for a friendly settlement, and had done everything in his power to secure it, he was not the man to sit down helplessly in face of such a situation as had now arisen. He felt there was no alternative for him but to bring the necessary action against the heritors to have them ordained to build the new Church. The small real rent heritors strenuously opposed the application to the Court on the grounds, first, that the peculiar circumstances in connection with its early history put Shettleston in a different position from other parish churches, and second, that by repairing the old building the erection of a new Church would be rendered unnecessary.

A prolonged litigation followed. Eventually the decision of the Court was announced and it was found to be in favour of the minister of Shettleston on every point. It was decreed that the heritors were solely responsible, that a new Church must be built to accomodate 1,200 people, and that the plans should be lodged forthwith.

This was one step to success, but the trouble was not yet at an end. The first plans submitted by the heritors to the Court were of a barn-like structure of the plainest description, their contention being that they were responsible only for giving the necessary space and not for providing a suitable place of worship. This also was successfully contested by Mr. White, the Court deciding that the heritors were bound to provide a suitable and comfortable place of worship such as any modern congregation possessing the requisite means would desire to erect. This marked another stage in the protracted proceedings; but even after the Church was built and ready for use a further obstacle was raised at the last moment. Political and local feeling still ran high, and an attempt was made to prevent the opening of the Church by refusing to give up the key. Another application had to be made to the Sheriff, who granted the necessary authority to " open and shut lockfast places."

At last, however, on August 19th, 1903, the new Church at Shettleston was actually opened. In a newspaper report it was said that " in spite of threats of opposition on the part of the heritors the new parish church was opened and dedicated by public worship without disturbance of any kind." The rumours which had been in circulation brought a large number of visitors, and the

Church was filled in every part when Mr. White preached the opening sermon. It was the last chapter in a long and at times bitter controversy, but it also marked the opening of a new period of prosperity in a successful and memorable ministry.

There was an interesting and fruitful sequel to the long dispute. In one point after another Mr. White had triumphed in his contest with the heritors, and now the Church had been built entirely by them. At the very first stage, however, as already explained, the congregation, on his initiative, had subscribed a considerable sum of its own towards the building scheme. As the Court, to whom the minister had been compelled to appeal, had decreed that the heritors must bear the whole cost of the new Church, this sum of money was still on hand. Large centres of population had been growing up in the districts of Tollcross and Carntyne within the parish of Shettleston and Mr. White, impressed by the growing needs of the new areas, turned his attention to them and initiated a movement for the establishment of a church in each of them. This was entirely a Church extension movement depending on voluntary effort, and the money which had been raised by the congregation of Shettleston for the building of their own new Church, but of which the heritors had not availed themselves, was therefore applied to the building of two daughter churches within the parish. So Mr White, who set out originally to build one church in Shettleston, was actually the means of building three, and these remain in the parish as permanent memorials of his ministry the Churches of Shettleston itself, of St. Margaret's, Tollcross and of Carntyne. It seems almost like a romance of history.

Under the happier conditions now prevailing in the ecclesiastical situation in Scotland it would will be impossible for a state of affairs to arise such as that which disturbed the parish of Shettleston through those stormy years. The matter, however, must not be judged in the light of the present but in the light of the past. Mr. White had to face the problem as he then found it and with the means then at his disposal. In view of the opposition aroused, and the keen feeling which prevailed, he had his critics and detractors in plenty. Yet he never swerved from what he felt to be the course of duty. While he carried the Presbytery of Glasgow along with him and had their moral support, he was left largely to fight his own battle. And the spectacle of this young minister, in the early years of his first pastorate, waging single-handed in the public gaze a warfare which even experienced warriors might have dreaded, was sufficient to appeal to the imagination. He might be condemned by his opponents as ruthless and relentless in the pursuit of his purpose, but they were constrained to admit, and even to admire, the ability and resource, the determination and the unfaltering confidence with which he pressed to his goal.

Photo: Lafayette]   *[Glasgow*

CARNTYNE PARISH CHURCH

Photo: Lafayette]   *[Glasgow*

TOLLCROSS (ST. MARGARET'S) PARISH CHURCH

In spite of all the prejudice and misunderstanding with which he had to contend he never wavered, and friend and foe alike were impressed by the calm, cool manner in which he bore himself through all the anxious and trying period. Not a few were ready to predict that the young minister who came through such an ordeal displaying talents so unusual in their range, and a personality with such a note of leadership, must be destined for a great part in the life of the Church at large in the coming years. And they prophesied even better than they knew, as the subsequent course of his life has so abundantly proved.

Time and again during those troublous years Mr. White was approached with invitations from important vacancies. Some of his friends, also, were anxious that he should seek an easier sphere. A layman in a letter written when the controversy was at its height wrote : " I see your troubles are not proving less and your life is being worried away. You should preach from the text, ' Consider Him which endured such contradiction of sinners.' We have a vacancy in ———— Free Church (an influential charge). Say the word ! "

All the entreaties of his friends, however, and all the definite overtures made to him from other churches, were turned down with the remark that his congregation at Shettleston had stood true to him through all the controversy and he would stand by them and remain in Shettleston until their troubles were at an end. This he did, and his ministry in the parish, which continued for ten years, was very much more than a record of troubles and triumphs with the heritors. The new Church, which was crowded when Mr. White preached the opening sermon continued crowded until the close of his ministry. His preaching—fresh, forcible, practical and eloquent —attracted people of all classes. Outside the pulpit his influence was felt in many ways. The work of the congregation was thoroughly organised, the care of the young received special attention, new agencies were instituted and fresh life was imparted to every branch of congregational effort. It was a period of abounding activity which left its mark deep on the whole life of the parish. The old animosities were gradually forgotten in the fruitful work of the subsequent years.

Some interesting incidents of the Shettleston ministry may be recalled both for their humour and for the light they throw on the manner of man the young minister was in his first charge. Not many months after he took up duty at Shettleston a marriage party arrived at the Manse one evening. The bridegroom was somewhat under the influence of drink, and Mr. White remonstrated with him only to find that he was inclined to be rather insolent. Finally Mr. White refused to perform the marriage ceremony and advised the bridal party to go away and get the bridegroom sobered up a bit. He told them he had an engagement in the city and would be back at the manse at

10.30 p.m., and if the bridegroom was then in a fit condition he would proceed with the marriage. There was considerable protest against this suggestion but Mr. White was adamant. At 10.30 the party returned with the bridegroom somewhat recovered. The young minister was still objecting when the bride broke in piteously—" O, Mr. White, will ye no mairry us ? I'm clean affronted afore oor Paisley freens. We've no' had oor tea yet, an' the pie is bein' wasted." The marriage was performed, but Mr. White's attitude was not without its effect.

During his early ministry in Shettleston Mr. White sought to brighten the rather sombre order of service. Gradually and prudently he introduced a more musical, more interesting form of worship. Quite naturally this did not appeal to some of the members who had been long accustomed to things as they were. At last one old woman, taking matters into her own hands, went to the manse to protest. After lodging her complaint at great length she finished up breathlessly—" In fac', Maister White, if it werena for Maggie an' the weans (Mrs. White and the children) ye wad be in the Roman Catholic Church."

The minister not only enjoyed the joke but he finally convinced the woman of his leanings towards the Church of Rome when he asked her to post for him a letter in the village. This letter (which merely contained a list of praise for the following Sunday), was addressed to Professor Cooper !

DR. JOHN WHITE

In the old vestry at Shettleston one Sunday morning some of the elders, including the Session Clerk, were present before the service while the minister was revising the list of praise with the organist. There was a knock at the door and a member of the congregation entered. He wished to arrange for a baptism and, when asked if he would not bring his child to church he refused. Mr. White was very busy at the time with so many engagements that he could not say at once what evening he would be able to go to the house to perform the baptism. The man got a little irritated and remarked that he had a good mind to " lift his lines." All the time this conversation had been going on Mr. White had been busy with the organist. When the lifting of lines was mentioned he turned to the Session Clerk, " Mr. ——— , give this gentleman his lines." And then in the same breath he remarked to the organist, " Mr. ——— , we will take No. 176 for the last Hymn."

The incident had a happy sequel. The man became one of Mr. White's most enthusiastic supporters and a very useful member of the Church.

It was not within his own congregation alone that Mr. White's influence was felt. He was in a very real sense the minister of the parish, as the people, irrespective of their own Church connection, went to him with their troubles and difficulties. Not the least moving of the tributes paid to him when he came to leave Shettleston were from members of other Churches whom he had made friends for life by his counsel in perplexing situations and his sympathy and kindness in days of bereavement.

The circumstances which led to his being called from Shettleston must, however, be reserved for the next chapter dealing with South Leith.

CHAPTER VII

SOUTH LEITH

It was not only without any desire on Mr. White's own part, or on the part of the congregation, that he was appointed to the parish of South Leith, but it was even done without his knowledge. The circumstances require some explanation, for the situation at the time had become one of such acute difficulty as to constitute a grave problem, involving not only local interests but also the welfare of the Church at large.

South Leith, one of the historic parishes of the Church of Scotland, with a record of many distinguished ministries through the centuries of its existence, had been raised to the position of having the largest congregation in Scotland, with a membership of over three thousand. The increase of its communion roll and the development of its life and activity had been due in no small measure to the long, devoted and vigorous ministry of Dr. James Mitchell, who was Moderator of the General Assembly in 1901. Unfortunately after Dr. Mitchell's retirement from South Leith on December 30th, 1903, the congregation were unable to agree as to the appointment of a successor within the six months' period allowed by the rules of the Church. The right of appointment was therefore no longer vested in the congregation but fell *tanquam jure devoluto* to the Presbytery. Two petitions very largely signed, for two different candidates, were thereafter submitted but, in view of the wide and strange divergence of opinion manifested by these petitions, the Presbytery considered it unwise to give effect to either of them. It was felt that the only wise course was to appoint some one whose name had not been before the congregation in any way.

Such a situation would in any case have required delicate handling, but this was more than ever necessary when the peace and prosperity of the largest congregation in the Church were at stake. The Presbytery of Edinburgh, however, were wisely guided in the matter. It was recognised that only a strong man would be equal to the emergency, and they turned to "White of Shettleston" as one supremely fitted for the position. It is no secret that for this wise choice the Presbytery were indebted to two of the prominent figures in the Church—Dr. Archibald Scott of St. Georges, the "leader" of the General Assembly, and Dr. Cameron Lees of St. Giles Cathedral, both of whom instinctively felt that in Mr. White there was the man for the hour. Dr. Scott declared that the members of Presbytery, "ought to congratulate themselves that they had got a man who was eminently fitted to maintain the high traditions of the Church of South Leith. He could assure them that their brother had a

very fine record, alike as a clergyman and a man
of great tact and commonsense. Mr. White
had found Shettleston Church in a very low
condition, and had made it one of the handsomest
in the whole Church. He had built two Churches
besides the Parish Church, and had finished the
erection of spacious Church halls. Then, he was
not only a well-read man but he had travelled considerably, having visited Central Europe, Greece,
Palestine, Egypt and Canada, and thereby
gathered much into a very thoughtful mind."
So impressed by the testimony from all quarters
were the members of Presbytery that the appointment was made immediately and with entire
unanimity.

To Mr. White the news of his election came as
a great surprise. Dr. Scott had written to tell
him that it was proposed to put forward his name
in the Presbytery but the letter was addressed
to the Manse at Shettleston, which, however,
was closed at the time, as Dr. White and his family
were away for their summer holiday at Arisaig.
The first information therefore he received was
a telegram which reached him at Arisaig stating :
" Presbytery have unanimously appointed you
to South Leith and have adjourned till Saturday.
Very urgent that we proceed at once."

This was, indeed, a bolt from the blue. Mr.
White had previously refused to allow his name to
be considered in connection with the vacancy, but
the circumstances now bore quite a different
complexion. It was no longer a case of being

asked to become a candidate ; it was a call from the Presbytery of Edinburgh to step in and save the situation. The official intimation of his appointment was followed by most cordial and pressing letters from Dr. Scott, Dr. Mitford Mitchell and other Church leaders, including Dr. James Mitchell the former minister of South Leith. Dr. Mitchell wrote :

" I must send a line to express my great gratification that you are to be my successor at South Leith. . . . I was devoutly thankful when I found that yours was the name which was likely to be put forward. I have heard so much of your good work at Shettleston and so much of you personally that I rejoice unfeignedly in your appointment. I have already done and will continue to do all in my power with my old friends on both sides to lay aside these temporary misunderstandings and to unite in favour of so good a man."

The announcement of the appointment was received in Glasgow and the West of Scotland with mixed feelings. There was regret at the prospective loss of a young minister who had already proved his mettle and had given such promise of future distinction. But there was also a certain pride that he had been chosen for so great a task. And there was certainly complete unanimity that no better choice could have been made for the difficult and delicate position. Letters poured in upon Mr. White from all quarters. Principal Story, his former teacher, wrote:

DR. JOHN WHITE

" The University,
" Glasgow,
" *July* 29, 1904.

" DEAR MR. WHITE,

" I have observed your appointment to South Leith with much pleasure. It is a very important charge and one for which your experience at Shettleston and your abilities in general qualify you extremely well. I wish you a long and happy ministry there.

" Very truly yours,
" (*Signed*) R. HERBERT STORY."

Dr. T. B. W. Niven of Pollokshields, who was Moderator of the General Assembly in 1906, wrote :

" Pollokshields,
" *July* 29, 1904.

" MY DEAR WHITE,

" Accept my warm congratulations on your most satisfactory appointment to South Leith. It must be very gratifying to you to have received it in the way you have. It is a splendid sphere and a most interesting charge. No man could be more worthy of it, after the admirable work you have done in Shettleston. I trust that you may have a long, happy and useful ministry in your new parish. We shall part with you from Glasgow with much regret. We cannot easily afford to lose so energetic and so judicious a co-Presbyter. But we may be very thankful to have had your valuable help so long, and our best wishes will be with you in your future career.

" Please offer my congratulations to Mrs. White. I trust she may find the change a very satisfactory one.

" Most truly yours,
" (*Signed*) T. B. W. NIVEN."

From Dr. Pearson McAdam Muir of Glasgow Cathedral (who was Moderator of the General Assembly in 1910) there came the following :

" *September* 12, 1904.

" DEAR MR. WHITE,

" Better late than never. I have intended for weeks to write you a few words of congratulation on your appointment to South Leith. The Presbytery of Edinburgh have shown remarkable wisdom in their action. Both they and the parish of South Leith have reason to be glad that their troubles have ended so happily. I cannot imagine any one whose appointment will give more thorough satisfaction to all concerned. Shettleston and Glasgow have reason to lament, but when the good of the Church is so evident they can only concur, however reluctantly. (It may even be that one or two heritors may breathe more freely !) I most cordially wish you all prosperity in your new charge.

" With kindest regards,
" Very sincerely yours,
" (*Signed*) P. McA. MUIR."

Mr. White's settlement at South Leith took place on September 27, 1904, the induction service being followed by a dinner in the Queen's Hotel, which was attended by a company of over 150, including, in addition to leading Churchmen, many of the foremost men in the public life of the community. There were several references to Mr. White's appointment as being a happy settlement of the " Eastern crisis," and one of the most significant speeches was made by Mr. W. Asher, S.S.C., who proposed the toast of " The Presbytery of Edinburgh." A few months previously Mr. Asher had appeared at the bar of the Presbytery pleading for the appointment of one of the ministers whose names had been before the congregation, but he now remarked that perhaps the Presbytery of Edinburgh could have rendered no greater service to the Church of Scotland than by appointing Mr. White to succeed Dr. Mitchell.

The proceedings at the induction dinner lasted for four hours, and almost immediately thereafter there was a congregational meeting in the Church to welcome the new minister, the crowded attendance and the eager enthusiasm making the evening a memorable one.

On the following Sunday, Mr. White was introduced to the congregation by the Rev. Dr. Donald Macleod, of the Park Church, Glasgow, the Editor of *Good Words*. After preaching from the text Hebrews, vi, 5, Dr. Macleod congratulated the congregation on their new minister and said that the task of introducing him was one which he undertook with all his heart. He continued—" I have known him and seen him both personally and through his work. A distinguished scholar, which his University career shows, he has proved himself a peculiarly earnest and energetic minister of a parish. He is a man of force and strong character, a man who finds and sees what ought to be done, and when he sees it ought to be done, take my word for it, it will be done. He is not easily kept back from duty. He is a splendid organiser and inspirer of work among others. I know you will find him a blessing. In the parish he has left he has done extraordinary work, both in amount and character, amid difficulties that might have deterred many a man and frightened many a man. He has left that parish changed as no one who knew it a few years ago would have believed possible. In spite of enormous difficulties, by sheer force of purpose and great tact, he erected there a new parish church much required. Besides that he has erected two or three subsidiary churches that are now doing splendid work in the parish. To do work of that kind means a man who has much in him and you will find that he has it in him. You will know that you have got in him a kind and wise counsellor, a delightful man, and the more you know him the more you will like him. To use a common phrase, he is a good fellow, in the best sense of the term. You will also find in him a pastor who will help you in all the most serious moments of your life, and you will also have an organiser who will carry out carefully thought-out schemes. You have got a guide you can trust. Support him and help him, and you will find good done in this great parish and congregation for which you will be thankful. I know Mr. White and love him, and when you know him you will love him too."

At the evening service, when the new minister preached his first sermon, the Provost, Magistrates and Town Council, wearing their official robes and accompanied by their leading officials, were present and the Church was crowded until many had to be content with standing room. Dr. Donald Macleod sat at the Communion Table and read the Lessons. Mr. White preached from the text, " Now I beseech you, brethren, for the Lord Jesus Christ's sake, and for the love of the Spirit, that ye strive together with me in your prayers to God for me." (Romans xv, 30.)

The ministry so auspiciously inaugurated soon made its influence felt not only in the congregation but throughout the whole community. Mr. White's preaching, as at Shettleston, made an immediate impression. Some of his sermons on occasions of local or national importance were specially notable. A great discourse on Nelson delivered in the year of the Nelson centenary was afterwards published at the urgent request of Professor James Cooper. One of his earliest discourses (delivered at the week night service)

SOUTH LEITH PARISH CHURCH

dealt in the most searching and comprehensive manner with the question of charities and the methods of relief in time of unemployment, and it was the means of placing on a new basis the whole arrangements of the congregation for the care of its poor and the giving of aid in times of sickness and distress. Some years later, in a sermon before the Town Council, he dealt powerfully with the problem of social wreckage and he further evinced his interest in social reform by submitting in the South Leith Magazine for 1911 some practical suggestions for Insurance against Unemployment. In thus anticipating what the State has subsequently undertaken he wrote : " This is a problem that has to be met and answered. It is not satisfactory to leave the unemployed, who have reached the end of their resources, to the care of the Church and the Charity Organizations. It is not fair to the Church, it is not fair to the unemployed."

Before he had been very long in South Leith Mr. White was convinced as to the necessity for the reconstruction of the Church Halls in order that there might be sufficient and suitable accommodation for the work of the congregation. He brought the matter at once before the Session and urged the desirability of proceeding without delay. As a large expenditure was involved, some of the members of Session were inclined to hesitate, but the minister assured them that the amount would soon be raised, and he had the satisfaction of seeing the new halls opened, amply equipped and fully used, and, in a short time, entirely cleared of debt.

Perhaps the great feature of his ministry, however, was the celebration of the Tercentenary of the Church. He was the first to bring to the notice of the congregation the fact that three hundred years of its history as a Reformed Parish Church would be completed in June, 1909, and he recommended that this should be made the occasion of a public celebration. A week-day service was held in the Church, attended by the Provost, Magistrates and Town Councillors, members of the Trinity House, Parish Council, School Board, and representatives of other public bodies, and by ministers of the several daughter Churches of South Leith, viz., St. Thomas' ; St. John's ; Abbey ; St. Paul's ; Restalrig and St. Mungo's. Mr. White preached the Tercentenary sermon and afterwards presided at a public luncheon. It was a great occasion, not only in the history of South Leith parish but in the life of the whole community, and it made a profound impression generally.

There was one amusing circumstance which deserves to be told. A printed order of service which had been issued for Commemoration Day contained a curious printer's error which somehow had escaped correction in the proof reading. Consequently the last line of the " Te Deum Laudamus : "

" O Lord in Thee have I trusted ; let me never be confounded," was given as : " O Lord

in Thee have I trusted ; let men ever be confounded."

Those were the days of militant suffragists, and
someone suggested that the printer's devil had
been at work !

On the following Sunday special Communion
Services were held, when there were 3,500 com-
municants, each of whom received a special
communion token which had been struck in
commemoration of the centenary. The entire
proceedings were a great success, and congratulations to the minister came from Church leaders
and many others. The Session of South Leith
also conveyed to him a special appreciation which
had been proposed by Provost Malcolm Smith,
carried with acclamation and ordered to be recorded in the Session Minutes. It contained an
expression of gratitude to Mr. White, " for his
conspicuous services in connection with the Tercentenary of the Church, for his initiation of
the various celebrations in connection with this
important event in its history, and for the eloquence and successful organisation with which he
had carried these out to the entire satisfaction,
not only of the congregation, but also of the
people of Leith."

A Tercentenary Bazaar was subsequently held,
and in connection with it a four page leaflet was
issued which marked a great advance on the
stereotyped and unattractive leaflets so often
published on behalf of Church Funds. On the
outside there was a picture of a peal of bells over
which there was printed :

while within there was a bright, cogent statement, of the objects of the Bazaar. "The chief object," it was said, " is to raise a sum of money to defray the cost of the Church Halls, 77 Duke Street. The cost of the Halls with some necessary furnishings is over £2,000. The Halls were opened on November 12, 1907, and are giving great satisfaction. They are already being taxed to their utmost to provide accommodation for our many church organisations. There is a large Upper Hall with side rooms ; two Lesser Halls ; Session Room and Committee Rooms on the ground floor.

" This year is our Church Tercentenary ; in 1609 the Church of St. Mary was constituted, by Act of Parliament, the Parish Church of South Leith in place of Restalrig which was ruinous. A year of such importance in the life of a Church that has bulked largely in the annals of the town of Leith, that has played its little side part in the history of the nation, that still possesses the subtle fascination of holding the affections of all who, at any time, have been associated with it, should not go unmarked.

" We appeal to every member and adherent of South Leith to undertake the responsibility of making this Bazaar a complete success. We also appeal to the Christian liberality of our many friends."

The result was a great success financially and otherwise. The necessary sum was raised, and the influence of the effort otherwise was helpful in many ways to the best interests of the congregation.

Always a glutton for work, Mr. White, despite the burden of his great congregation, was ready to take his share in philanthropic and charitable efforts in the community, and in connection with many of these his sound judgment, business experience and knowledge of men and of affairs proved of the utmost value. It was said of him that the people generally looked to him not merely as the minister of his own congregation but as the minister of Leith. At the same time he was steadily becoming a power in the Church Courts, and had been appointed Clerk to the Church of Scotland Committee in conference with the United Free Church; but his connection with the Union movement must be dealt with in another chapter. It should be said here, however, that one of his first public pronouncements on the Union question was made from the pulpit of South Leith in a great sermon preached from its pulpit at Christmas, 1909, and subsequently published in the Church magazine.

More and more the eyes of the Church were fixed on the minister of South Leith, and he was hailed on every hand as one of the Church leaders of the future. South Leith was justifiably proud of his great and growing reputation, but his ministry there was destined to be a comparatively brief one. Before he had been seven years in the parish it became apparent that he would not be allowed to settle down permanently. Matters came to a crisis in the early months of 1911. On one day Mr. White received two invitations—one was to go out to Montreal as minister of St. Paul's, the leading Presbyterian Church in Canada, and the other to return to his native city of Glasgow to fill the historic pulpit of the Barony church. The story is told of how the Glasgow people forestalled the Canadians. Learning from an official in the Church Offices that a deputation on behalf of the Montreal Church would be at South Leith Manse next morning at eleven o'clock, the Glasgow deputation travelled early and appeared at the Manse at ten o'clock—an excellent example of Glasgow enterprise. It would be interesting to speculate how the whole course of Scottish Church history might have been different if the Glasgow deputation had not forestalled that from Montreal and succeeded in keeping Dr. White in Scotland.

In connection with this incident an amusing story is told by Dr. White's daughter, Mrs. Glen. It was the time when there was a great craze for a game known as " Diabolo " which consisted in whirling on a string, fastened to two sticks, a small spool-shaped object so as to balance it on the string, toss it in the air, and catch it again on the string. Mrs. Glen recalls how, on the particular morning referred to, a most imposing deputation had just been ushered into the Library in the South Leith Manse. " We children," she says, " tremendously impressed, were peeping out from various corners of the hall. The maid had gone in search of Dr. White and drawn a blank in the study. My elder brother, anxious to help, gave a loud and penetrating shout from his coign of vantage, unfortunately near the library door—" Pater's up in the telephone room, practising ' Diabolo.' " " This, I may add," continues Mrs. Glen, " did not weigh against Dr. White with the deputation."

The picture of a minister calmly practising the game of " Diabolo " while two competing deputations were making frantic efforts to induce him to accept a call is one not likely to be forgotten.

Mr. White was not allowed to leave South Leith without being assured of the enthusiastic appreciation of his ministry and without carrying with him tangible tokens of the esteem of the people. Provost Malcolm Smith, in making the presentation, remarked that if the congregation were assured they would get as good a man as Mr. White they would be very glad to hand over to the Presbytery again the duty of selecting a minister. Mrs. White was specially honoured, and in acknowledging the presentation made to her, Mr. White said that he had not been accustomed to speaking in public of what she had done in the Church and the parish, but if ever a minister's wife deserved recognition Mrs. White did. During the years they had been in Leith the manse had kept an open door to the parishioners, and he could not speak too highly of all she had accomplished. Presentations were also made to

Mr. and Mrs. White from the Sunday School teachers and others. What may be regarded as a permanent memorial of Mr. White's ministry must not be overlooked. When the new Gallery screen was erected in 1911 the initials " D.L." and " J.W." were inscribed. The former were those of the Rev. David Lindsay, who was minister in 1609 when South Leith became the Parish Church, and the latter those of the Rev. John White, who was minister at the Tercentenary in 1909.

Thus had the conditions changed during the seven brief but eventful years. The minister who had gone to South Leith, not as the choice of the congregation but as the nominee of the Presbytery, had more than justified his nomination and had so commended himself by his personality and work as to unite all the different sections into one harmonious whole. It was with the appreciation and esteem of the whole congregation as well as of the community that he left for his new sphere in which as " White of the Barony," he was to become best known to the Church and to the world at large.

CHAPTER VIII

THE BARONY CHURCH, GLASGOW

In order to understand the significance of the unanimous call presented to Dr. White from the Barony Church, Glasgow, in May, 1911, it is necessary to bring into review the history and traditions which have made " the Parish Kirk of the Barony of Glasgow " (to use its ancient full-dress title) a name in all the earth. Though it cannot claim any pre-Reformation record it holds a foremost place among the great churches of Scotland. To summarise the salient facts of its story, with even the mere narration of historical facts or outstanding personalities, may help those who possess no intimate knowledge of its history to visualise its meaning for " the Christian good of Scotland."

In the history of the Barony Church, according to the changing location of its worship, the following three periods stand out clearly as marking its progressive influence in the city of Glasgow and beyond.

(1) The Crypt of Glasgow Cathedral (St. Mungo's or The High Church), 1595-1799.

(2) The Old Barony Church, 1799-1889.

(3) The present Church, from 1889 to the present day.

The growth of population in the city of Glasgow, and especially in its landward area, in the years succeeding the Scottish Reformation of 1560 was such as to necessitate some corresponding increase in the provision of Christian ordinances and pastoral supervision. To this end those resident in the Barony (or landward portion " without the town "), as distinct from the city (or urban portion of the parish of Glasgow), were assigned " a Kirk of their own," but instead of erecting a new Church the Crypt of the Cathedral was set apart in 1595 for their use as a place of worship. This was one of the first results of what seemed for the time an end of the struggle between Presbytery and Prelacy in the Scottish Church.

A visitor to the Cathedral to-day may rightly admire its architecture, but is left wondering how services could have been conducted for almost two centuries in the dismal precincts of its many-pillared crypt. In an era of more regular attendance at divine worship than is now customary, it must have been crowded to the point of discomfort, and the more so as the city enlarged its boundaries. The description given by Sir Walter Scott in " Rob Roy," though familiar, bears repetition. " We entered a small, low-arched door, secured by a wicket, which a grave-looking person seemed on the point of closing and descended several steps, as if into the funeral vaults beneath the Church. It was even so ; for in these sub-terranean precincts, why chosen for such a purpose I know not, was established a very singular place of worship. Conceive . . . an extensive range of low-browed, dark, and twilight vaults, such as are used for sepulchres in other countries, and had long been dedicated to the same purpose in this, a portion of which was seated with pews, and used as a church. The part of the vaults thus occupied, though capable of containing a congregation of many hundreds, bore a small proportion to the darker and more extensive caverns which yawned around what may be termed the inhabited space. In those waste regions of oblivion, dusky banners and tattered escutcheons indicated the graves of those who were, doubtless, ' princes in Israel ' . . . Surrounded by these receptacles of the last remains of mortality, I found a numerous congregation engaged in the act of prayer." Thus did " the Wizard of the North " weave into his narrative his own impressions of a Barony Kirk service of the late eighteenth century, using Sir Francis Osbaldistone as the medium of his thoughts. The shadow of Andrew Fairservice ever lingers among the pillars, and even now we would fain imagine with Scott that Rob Roy on occasion visited the crypt, albeit his purpose was not always to pray.

Of the ministers whose work and worth adorned the Barony Church of the Crypt none are held in higher honour than Zachary Boyd and Donald Cargill, both of whom took full share in the troublous period of the seventeenth century. Among the interesting documents still preserved in the Barony is the " Presentation for Ye Barony Kirk of Glasgow to Mr. Zacharias Boyd, Minister, subscribed by ye Archbishop of Glasgow, Dean, Chaptour and Consentary within written. February 2nd, 1625." Dr. Lang's comment on this document may be quoted—" An illustration of the curious jumble of Prelacy and Presbytery which marked the period." Distinguished in learning, he was elected Lord Rector of Glasgow University on three occasions, and in 1643, while still minister of the Barony, he held the office of Vice-Chancellor. His labours as a paraphrast led to a recommendation by the General Assembly of 1647 that he should " be at the pains to translate the other Scripturall Songs in meeter." The result, however, does not seem to have commended itself either to the Assembly or to the people. Yet his name stands high in the Barony records, not for academic honours nor yet for Scripture paraphrases, but chiefly because with unflinching courage he upheld the cause of truth as he saw it, even before the presence of Oliver Cromwell. After the defeat of the Scots at Dunbar, Cromwell, with his army of Independents, marched westward to Glasgow. The magistrates and ministers made a prudent withdrawal from the city, content to await the next turn of events. But the minister of the Barony withstood the Protector to his face, " railing against him " in his very presence when he attended service in the Cathedral or " Hie Kirk." " Shall I pistol the scoundrel ? " asked Cromwell's Secretary. " No, no, we will manage him some other way," answered Cromwell, and immediately proceeded to invite the preacher to dine with him the same evening. The dinner was followed by family worship conducted by Cromwell himself, who gave his famous three hours' prayer " from midnight until three in the morning," from which " Mr. Zacharias," as Boyd was usually termed, rose weary in knee but welded in heart to the friendship of Cromwell.

The bitter religious strife occasioned by the restoration of Prelacy under Charles II brought into prominence Donald Cargill, the next minister of the Barony. Resenting the intrusion of alien forms of worship imposed by royalty, he proceeded to denounce the reigning king. The stubborn defence raised by Richard Cameron and Donald Cargill in the movement for the honour of " Christ's Crown and Covenant " is well known. It is to Donald Cargill, martyr-minister of the Barony, that one of the most famous of Scottish regiments owes its origin. When the sons of the present minister and he himself went forth in the day of the ordeal it was not surprising to find that the regiment of their choice was the Scottish Rifles, which in 1920 was re-named " The Cameronians (Scottish Rifles)" in acknow- ledgment of their worthy sacrifice and service on many fronts during the War. Dr. MacLean Watt, minister of Glasgow Cathedral, and an authority on the history of the Scottish regiments, in a protest against a proposal to obliterate the name of the Cameronians writes : " It perpetuates certain old habits which remind us of its origin. The band and pipers do not play on Sundays when marching with the regiment, remembering the strictness of the Covenanters in observance of the Sabbath. When attending Church parade, the men are armed, carrying their rifles, in commemoration of the custom of the Covenanters to have sentries placed around the conventicles in days of persecution among the hills. The men carry a Bible to Church as did the Covenanters to their gatherings. There is thus in this regiment a continuity of Scottish tradition and sentiment of a specially unique kind —a pathetic memorial of the courage and devoted fidelity which illumined one of the grimmest periods of our national story ; and this speaks always to the youngest recruit of duty and the significance of the corps."

The Barony Church has good reason to be proud of its association with Donald Cargill of the Covenant.

The comparative calm which supervened on this era of tumult was followed by a period of less colourful activity in the Barony story. Among those who during the eighteenth century ministered in the Barony it is sufficient to mention only Dr. John Hamilton and the Rev. Laurence Hill. Dr. Hamilton had the unique experience of being translated from the Barony in the Crypt to the Inner High Church or Cathedral. Literally a promotion from downstairs, it was later followed by his further appointment as Moderator of the

General Assembly in 1766. With reference to Dr. Hamilton's translation it may be explained that for almost two hundred years three congregations worshipped in the present Cathedral : the Barony, as we have seen, in the Crypt ; the parishioners of the Inner High (represented by the Cathedral congregation of to-day) in the choir ; and those of the Outer High (represented by the present St. Paul's congregation) in the nave. In 1836 a new church, St. Paul's, erected on the site of the present Royal Technical College, was set apart for the worship of the Outer High congregation of the nave. The transfer of the Barony congregation from the crypt had taken place some thirty-six years previously. Of Mr. Laurence Hill it need only be said that his family name is one which can claim an honourable connection with the city of Glasgow, of which he was enrolled as an honorary burgess, an honour given to few representatives of the church.

The passing of the eighteenth century rings down the curtain on this notable period of two centuries of the " Kirk o' The Barony." For, on June 28, 1799, the foundation stone of a new church was laid, and in the following year the congregation moved out from the laigh (i.e., low) kirk beneath the Cathedral to their new home close to the present main entrance to Glasgow Necropolis. The new church—long since demolished and now always termed " The old Barony " —was in no sense a thing of beauty. On the contrary, it revealed a decadent stage in the taste of ecclesiastical architecture. Of the old Barony the Earl of Derby is reported to have said, " I have once seen an uglier."

Internally it was little better than externally. The pulpit stair was so narrow that in the case of a burly figure like that of Dr. Norman Macleod it was necessary to attempt it sideways. A plaster roof, which had been an eyesore to some, was later on removed for the sake of ventilation, but some ardent Barony members resented the change. " It was a bonnie roof," said one of the malcontents, " wi' its strings like raisin strings from a' the corners running to the big rose in the centre." The seats, with few exceptions, were uncomfortably tight. A corpulent member once excused himself for irregular attendance by saying that he always returned from Church with a pain, not in his soul but in his stomach, because of the cramped position in which he had to sit in his pew.

Yet, when the worst has been said regarding its castellated facade and tower, its dim lighting, its uncomfortable pews, and its faulty ventilation, this also must be added. Its foundation stone, which now rests in the present noble building as the pedestal of the lectern, is a constant reminder that even the culpable neglect of beauty in wood and stone cannot for ever shut out the glory of God in the face of Christ or in the lives of His saints. On the upper surface of the stone are engraved names which cannot die——Burns, Black, Macleod, Lang——the four ministers of the old

Barony Church. In addition to the foundation stone and its iron box of contemporary documents, there can still be seen in the Barony Church such articles as the quaint three-legged seat which served the elder on duty at the collection plates in the vestibule of the old church and the simple baptismal bowl used for well nigh a hundred years. The ornate wooden pillars which flanked the two inner doors of the former church now stand on either side of the platform in the Church Hall. An artistic chair now on this platform, as also a fine suite of Chippendale chairs in the vestry, are further treasures from the historic past. " I glory," said Norman Macleod on one occasion, " in knowing that I have brought more souls to the knowledge of God their Father and of Jesus Christ their Elder Brother, under these old rafters than many a Bishop has done in the stateliest cathedral."

Dr. John Burns, who for four years prior to the death of Laurence Hill had served as assistant, was ordained in the Crypt of the Cathedral in 1773 and for sixty-six years maintained a ministry of gracious influence in the city, attaining at his death the venerable age of ninety-five years. During his long tenure of office as minister of the Church he was noteworthy for his advocacy of Foreign Mission enterprise in a day when the wider duty of the Church to the Nations received little support. He founded the first Sunday School in Scotland in the Calton district of Glasgow in 1775, soon after his admission to the charge, thus anticipating by five years the opening of Robert Raikes' famous school in Gloucester. No one is prouder of this priority of origin in Sunday School work than the present minister of the Barony, who, in expressing the welcome of the Glasgow Churches to some 4,000 delegates to the World's Sunday School Covention held in that city in June, 1924, referred to this Barony pioneer in the spiritual welfare of youth. Owing to the transfer in 1800 to the Old Barony, Dr. Burns had the distinction, later achieved by Dr. Marshall Lang, of serving the charge in a transition period of its history. Dr. Burns was the father of the first Lord Inverclyde.

In 1826 a young man, William Black, was ordained to Shettleston Parish, which holds premier place as " the eldest daughter of the Barony " among fully forty parishes which have been carved out of the one original parish. After a short ministry of only two years he was translated in 1828 to the Barony as Assistant and Successor to Dr. Burns, on whose death in 1839 he became minister of the charge. A story occasionally associated with other men, is still handed down to each Barony generation. " You'll be wearying for Dr. Burns' death, Mr. Black," they would say to him. With nimble wit, of which he was a master, he replied, " Not at all, I am only wearying for his *living*." Dr. William Black, " one of the largest hearted men who ever breathed," maintained the Barony tradition, and as he lay dying recommended Norman Macleod, already known

Photo : Lafayette

THE BARONY CHURCH, GLASGOW

[*Glasgow*

to the Barony congregation, as the one man fitted
to succeed him.

Dr. Norman Macleod's ministry of twenty-one
years (1851-1872) was the means of making
"The Barony" a household word in every
quarter of the land, and even "furth of Scotland."
Possessing many gifts of high culture, broad
humanity, wise leadership, and noble eloquence,
he enriched city and nation with the full influence
of his great personality. A pioneer in many
fields and the founder of "Good Words," he
is specially remembered in the Barony for his
efforts to supply the spiritual needs of the poor
and needy, while remaining to the end the friend
and confidant of those in high places. The
first congregational savings bank instituted by
him in 1852 still maintains a fruitful service
in the cause of thrift, while the "Moleskin
Kirk," as it was called, erected at first to accommo-
date working men and women in their work-a-day
garb, is now the church of a parish bearing his
name. In 1869 he was elected to the Moderator's
chair of the General Assembly, the first of four
successive ministers of the Barony to attain the
highest honour within the bestowal of the church.
The spirit of the man found expression in the
wealth of his message. Speaking for the last
time in the General Assembly, he said, "So long
as I have a good conscience towards God and
have His sun to shine on me, and can hear the
birds singing, I can walk across the earth with a
joyful and free heart. Let them call me 'broad.'

I desire to be broad as the charity of Almighty God, who maketh His sun to shine on the evil and on the good : who hateth no man, and who loveth the poorest Hindoo more than all their committees or all their Churches. But while I long for that breadth of charity I desire to be narrow—narrow as God's righteousness, which as a sharp sword can separate between eternal right and eternal wrong."

His successor, Dr. John Marshall Lang, built of a different mould and therefore equipped for a different task, continued the work begun by "the great Norman." While taking a prominent share in the public duties which, from the nature of their office, have fallen to all ministers of the Barony, his supreme work was the building of the present noble edifice. After many years of arduous labour in rousing enthusiasm for the project of a new and more worthy church, and in raising the large sum of about £30,000 entirely by voluntary effort, the present church was "dedicated to the glory of God and to His worship," on April 27, 1889. As a place of worship the Barony Church is now almost unequalled in Scotland for stateliness of structure and seemliness of furnishing. Designed by Sir John J. Burnet, who is now an architect of international fame, it has proved a worthy setting for great ministries. In 1900 Dr. Marshall Lang was appointed Principal of Aberdeen University. It was with a justifiable sense of pride that the Barony congregation in 1928 rejoiced to see his son, Dr. Cosmo Gordon Lang, then Archbishop of York, elevated to the high office of Archbishop of Canterbury and Primate of all England.

Dr. Marshall Lang was succeeded by Dr. Thomas Martin, whose monument is to be seen not in things made with hands but in the enduring affection which he won and maintained for eleven years in the Barony congregation. His outstanding gifts, amounting to genius, for pastoral work, were employed ungrudgingly and unceasingly for the upbuilding of a strong church life in the new church. To this end he laboured night and day, leaving no sphere of pastoral duty untouched by his gracious ministration. Under his ministry the congregation increased till, at his translation to Peebles in 1911, it had reached a total of 3,000 members. As to Dr. Martin there had come, as the heritage from his predecessor, the magnificent Barony Church, so in turn he was able to hand over in 1911 a congregation which, in numbers and service, was unequalled in the city. The future years were to reveal in what manner this historic past was to merge into a ministry with its centre and inspiration in the Barony Church, while its issues are in the coming re-united Church of Scotland. "When the Church renounces its past, it renounces its future." This dictum of Dr. White may serve as a fitting conclusion to the story of the Barony of Glasgow as it goes on to meet the dawning day.

CHAPTER IX

THE PREACHER AND PASTOR

" I am voicing the general opinion of your brethren in the ministry when I say that no one has ever received promotion with greater goodwill than you have on your appointment to this outstanding Church and parish." With these words the officiating minister on behalf of the Presbytery of Glasgow welcomed the Rev. John White on his induction to the Barony on Wednesday, June 7, 1911.

Dr. A. M. Maclean, of Paisley Abbey, in a speech at the luncheon which followed, said it sometimes happened that a minister was called to an important sphere of service not merely by the vote of a particular congregation but by the voice of the whole church. Such a call had recently transferred Dr. Wallace Williamson from St. Cuthbert's to St. Giles', and that day it had brought Mr. White from South Leith to the Barony. He believed that in the opinion of the whole church Mr. White was the one man best fitted to be the successor of the famous ministers who had given the Barony its unique position of influence in the city and the country.

Dr Wallace Williamson, probably with the story, quoted in the previous chapter, of Zachary Boyd and Oliver Cromwell in mind, remarked that, " he would like to see any modern Oliver Cromwell try to browbeat or drive from his purpose John White, once he had made up his mind as to the right thing to say and do."

The new minister in his acknowledgment confessed that while in the East hearts were as warm as in the West, he had a slight preference for the West, and for its quick and articulate sympathy. He came back to his native city, the great city of the West, with its intense life, its world-wide interests, its energetic Church life, its experimental social charities, its municipal enterprise and high civic ideals, and he was grateful for the opportunity of again sharing in the pulsating life of the great city of Glasgow.

One of the first important events in his ministry was the celebration of the centenary of the birth of Dr. Norman Macleod. It took place on June 9, 1912—the first anniversary of Mr. White's induction—and it was officially attended by the Town Council and other public bodies and also by the 5th Scottish Rifles, the regiment so intimately associated with the Barony.

Then came the celebration of the semi-jubilee of the opening of the present Barony Church in April, 1914, and the ministry so auspiciously opened was going from strength to strength. A few months later the country was in the throes of war with all its interruption of the ordinary routine of life.   In the Barony, as elsewhere, in the early days of stress and strain there were crowded pews, and the minister was stirred with indignation at the welter of blood into which the world had been cast by the ambition of the enemy. On one memorable Sunday in the course of a powerful sermon throbbing with righteous passion he suddenly exclaimed, " Damn the Kaiser," and the people, breaking for once the silence of the pew, gave vent to their feelings of strong approbation.   It was an unusual incident, but the circumstances were unprecedented.

Very soon Mr. White volunteered for service as a Chaplain, and he was for some months attached to the East Coast Defences, thereafter proceeding to France on August 23, 1915.   He was attached to the 5th Cameronians and afterwards to the 19th Infantry Brigade which included the Cameronians, and the fitness of this connection will be at once apparent from what has already been said regarding the intimate associations of this regiment with the Barony and its ministers.   It was his own Battalion which he had joined thirty-two years ago and in which three generations of his family had served.   It had at one time Dr. White as Chaplain and two of his sons, Captain M. K. White and Lieut. John Gardner White, as officers.   He served for two years at the front, winning golden opinions for his heroic and helpful service, and it is worthy of note that the one book he has found time to write in the course of his busy life is an account of the work of that regiment, which was published under the title " With the Cameronians."

His messages from the front, written oftentimes amid the din of bombardment, and interrupted by the claims of duty to the wounded and the dying, were read and treasured by his congregation. The fact that almost one thousand men from the Barony had responded to the country's call made him justly proud. " I have seen many of them here," he wrote in one of his letters, " and they are men to be proud of. It has been a great privilege to be of some little service to them. I never feel that I am doing a tithe of the work done by the poorest Tommy who is drudging and trudging through this tragic business." His diary from France issued monthly in the Barony Church magazine had many characteristic touches. In a reference to the Argyll and Sutherland Highlanders " swinging past " to the line, he said, " It was a Glasgow man, from the South side evidently, who amidst much laughter shouted to a French laddie as they were passing on—' A say, ma mannie, is it faur tae the Paisley Road Toll ? ' They were happy and perspiring for it was scorching hot, and they were returning to the trenches. To-night the aeroplanes are busy over the lines, and shells are bursting near them. One does not look for hell-fire so high up, but the world is turned upside down just now."

Soon after the outbreak of war the minister of the Barony and his wife were overtaken by sorrow in their own home when, on December 26, 1914, their youngest child, Margaret, a girl of twelve years, passed away after a brief illness. In later years Dr. White has comforted sorrowing parents with the comfort wherewith he himself was then enabled to take up again the daily tasks.

Another bereavement fell on the manse in August, 1917, when Lieut. John Gardner White, who had been transferred to the Royal Flying Corps, fell at the front after " successfully accomplishing a special mission over the German lines." The simple wooden cross erected by the enemy over his grave is now the treasured possession of Dr. White.

When Dr White returned from war service to resume his ministry he threw himself with all his ardour and energy into the work of the Barony, and his pulpit became more than ever his throne. Only those who have " sat under " him know how earnestly he has devoted himself to what is, after all, the main work of the Christian minister. The richness of his devotional exercises have been a subject of remark, and his preaching has been consistently true to the best traditions of the Scottish pulpit. " While carrying in every well measured phrase the marks of scholarship, his sermons have," it has been said, " made a ready appeal to the humblest of the congregation." His first sermon in the Barony was based on the text, " And the common people heard him gladly." It was a characteristic choice. His preaching often touches heights of eloquence and even of nobility ; it is massive and powerful and robust, but all the time it is suffused by an evangelical spirit, and there runs through it the practical note which brings it close to human hearts baffled by life's problems and burdened by its sorrows.

The Communion Service, conducted by Dr. White according to the time-honoured order of the Scottish Church, is always an impressive event in the Barony. On one occasion the visiting minister entered into a diffuse theological argument regarding the Sacrament. The following day Dr. White, in referring to this, while counselling one of his assistants, said " Remember the Communion Table is never the place for controversy on the meaning of Christ's death, but of contemplation of its glorious message for us. We must show Christ and Him only." Then he proceeded to tell the story of the artist who painted the Last Supper and portrayed a golden chalice in the hand of Christ; and when a brother craftsman extolled the exquisite beauty of the chalice the artist with one sweep of his brush blotted it out of the picture. " I wanted men to see the surpassing loveliness on the face of Christ," he exclaimed ," and you see only the chalice." Standing in front of his study fire Dr. White added, " Yes, not the cup but Christ." It was a lesson one assistant was not likely to forget.

The story is still told of an occasion when that great evangelist, Gipsy Smith, was conducting a special mission in Glasgow and, in connection

DR. JOHN WHITE

with it, held a series of lunch hour meetings for business men. At one of these Dr. White presided and gave the opening address, at the close of which Gipsy Smith rose and said in his own dramatic way, " Gentlemen, why ask me to come to Glasgow when you have a man like that? " It was one preacher of authentic gifts and power recognising the other.

No part of Dr. White's work has been more impressive or effective than the preparation of his young people for admission to the Communion. In the extensive work of the congregation among the young in numerous organisations he takes the keenest interest, but he always regards them merely as auxiliaries to the Church and not as substitutes for it. " There is no doubt," said Dr. White on one occasion, " that the education authorities are doing much by teaching the three R's, but we want the four R's—reading, writing, 'rithmetic, and religion." The Barony is a busy hive of industry and its Mission Institute in Black Street is a centre of aggressive evangelism in a needy district.

In a congregation of 3,000 members, not to speak of the multitude of adherents, it has naturally been impossible for Dr. White to attain his desire for periodical visitation of every home. He has gathered around him, however, in his two or three assistants, parish sisters and others, a body of helpers who, under his efficient supervision and perfect organisation, carry out the work. But his own pastoral service is of the

THE BARONY CHURCH. GLASGOW (Interior)

very highest value. No serious case is ever left unattended by himself personally. He has the instinct of a true pastor of souls. Not alone in the intimate hours of suffering and sorrow in the home are his ministrations exercised, but also in his weekly " consultations " in the vestry. Often on his arrival in the city from his public work in connection with the Church at meetings in Edinburgh or throughout the country he has gone straight from the railway train to the vestry to attend to the needs of his waiting parishioners.

The strain under which Dr. White had been working was revealed early in 1920, when he was laid aside with a severe attack of pneumonia, and for a time his life seemed to hang in the balance. Happily his strong constitution triumphed in the end, although he was unable for some time to resume his full ministry. The anxious solicitude of his people was an eloquent tribute to the place he had made for himself in all their hearts.

Another evidence of the relationship existing between Dr. and Mrs. White and the congregation was afforded on the occasion of the wedding of their daughter, Miss Lily White, to Mr. J. T. K. Glen of Glengowan, Caldercruix, on April 18, 1922. Handsome gifts were made to the bride by the Kirk Session and congregation and many of the Church agencies, while the crowds at the wedding in the Barony were almost unpre-cedented.

On the occasion of his ministerial semi-jubilee his former congregations at Shettleston and

South Leith united with the Barony in tributes of appreciation and the presentation of tangible tokens of regard. The money gift Dr. and Mrs. White set apart for the Memorial in the Barony to the boys of the congregation who had fallen in the war.

Two other honours must be specially mentioned. One was the conferment of the honorary degree of D.D. by his Alma Mater, the University of Glasgow, in June 24, 1920, and the other his appointment by the King as one of His Majesty's Chaplains in Scotland.

The Barony congregation at an enthusiastic meeting to welcome Dr. White on his return after his serious illness and to congratulate him on his academic honour, presented him with new pulpit robes and D.D. hood along with other gifts for himself and Mrs. White. His appointment as a Chaplain to the King was hailed with great satis-faction. As one writer put it—" It is said ' the King can do no wrong,' but there are occasions on which the aphorism is more conspicuously true than others and this is one of them." His Majesty's choice commanded universal approval.

In his relations with his assistants, now a goodly band of about forty, scattered all over the Church at home and abroad, Dr. White has always sought to impress the young men, at the formative period in their career, with a worthy conception of the ministerial office. By precept and example he has taught them many things they could never forget. More than one can recall how he was told not to say after reading the Scripture Lesson, " The Lord *add* His blessing." " The blessing is in the Word," emphasised Dr. White. " Why therefore pray for it as an addition ? It is sufficient to say, The Lord bless to us. . . ."

Hard working, efficient and loyal himself, he gave the young men trained under him the most valuable experience they could have desired, and their appreciation of what they learned from him is equalled only by the enduring bond of friendship which still links them to their former " Bishop." Among the presentations made to Dr. White in his Moderatorial year of 1925 was one from his former assistants. The gifts, consisting of a gold chalice, along with a gold Iona Cross for Mrs White, were handed over during the sittings of the General Assembly, when in one of the Committee rooms the Moderator appeared again as the " big brother," and gave a speech full of reminiscence and characteristic humour.

Some familiar stories are told in the Barony congregation. There was the old man waxing reminiscent of his long connection with the Church who exclaimed in the broadest Doric— " A hae sat under Doctor Norman, Doctor Marshall Lang, Doctor Martin and noo under John White, an' I'm still a Christian."

Another is of the Barony elder who had been asked by Dr. White in the absence of the assistants on holiday to read the Scripture Lesson. The

Old Testament passage was from the Book of Ecclesiastes, but as the Lectern Bible contains the Apocrypha the elder turned up by mistake the corresponding chapter in the Book of Ecclesiasticus. He read it unconcernedly from beginning to end to a mystified congregation.

One story relates to Dr. White himself. Always warmly interested in Foreign Missions, he took a leading part in the International Missionary Congress held in Glasgow in 1922, and at one of the sessions, when he had taken his place on the platform, a delegate from other lands enquired of his neighbour, " Who is the man like Caesar ? " The striking features of the Barony minister had recalled to one mind at least the lineaments of the Roman Emperor.

In the years of Dr. White's public work for the Church, when he has had to be absent frequently from his own pulpit, the loyalty of the Barony has never wavered. Time and again he has acknowledged the sympathetic support of his people and the heartening they have given him in his great endeavour. Thus minister and congregation alike have shared in the movement so vitally affecting the whole ecclesiastical and religious life of Scotland.

CHAPTER X

IN THE GENERAL ASSEMBLY

It is interesting to recall Dr. White's first appearance as a speaker on the floor of the General Assembly in which he was later on to become so great a figure. That first appearance of his was both characteristic and significant. It revealed the man as he was at an early stage of his career, and it seemed prophetic of the future.

Many ministers attend the Assembly regularly as opportunity offers throughout the whole course of their ministerial life without once intervening in the discussions. They leave the business to others and are content to go on merely giving silent votes. Even some who have afterwards become leaders have been slow in taking the first step, and have been long in lifting up their voice in the Assembly Hall. With Dr. White it was entirely otherwise.

In 1894—the year following his ordination and induction at Shettleston—he was returned as a member of the Assembly from the Presbytery of Glasgow, and before that Assembly closed he had made his first Assembly speech and been appointed to his first committee. It was not, however, a case of rushing in rashly against men of experience. It was the helpful contribution of a young man who was able to state the case of the younger ministers in a way which at once appealed to the leaders of the Court.

The Assembly had come to the appointment of the Probationers Committee, and when the names were announced Mr. White, rising in his place on an obscure bench, remarked that it seemed a strange proceeding that such a committee should be composed entirely of D.D.'s and other grave and reverend senior members of Assembly. It was the year when Principal Story was Moderator and, turning round in the Moderator's chair, the Principal gave his former student, who had so recently left his classes, a smile of encouragement as he proceeded to argue for the inclusion in the Committee of some members of Assembly who might naturally be expected to be more closely in touch with the young probationers. Dr. Marshall Lang, then minister of the Barony, who had been Moderator in the previous year, at once rose from his seat at the Table and said he welcomed the speech of the young minister of Shettleston and admitted the fairness and force of his argument. Dr. Lang concluded by proposing that Mr. White should be added to the committee. This, however, Mr. White protested was not what had been in his mind, but eventually, when it was decided to include several of the younger ministers, he agreed to be one of them.

This first public utterance by Dr. White in

the General Assembly was not in the form of a set speech. He spoke on the spur of the moment, thereby revealing one of the most conspicuous traits in his subsequent Assembly career—his readiness quickly and competently to grasp a situation and make a point. And his maiden speech in the Assembly was also like many others that have followed in that it was successful in accomplishing something.

With many men it is a long and laborious process to get into the spirit and the ways of Church Courts. Of Dr. White, however, it has been said that, " he took to the Assembly as a duck takes to the water." And it was not long before he was making his influence felt.

As early as 1913 he was taking an active part in the business of the Assembly. A special report had been submitted with certain new recommendations and dealing with the amendment of the Standing Orders. In the course of a long and involved discussion, in which many of the leaders took part, he succeeded in carrying the proposal for a quorum of thirty in the form which he suggested.

In the following year, 1914, for from then onwards he was a member almost continuously, he delivered what was described at the time as a rousing speech in which he dealt with the evils of intemperance, impurity and gambling, and said that the Reformation of to-day had to be social, affectional and ethical. "It was time," he said, " that the Church of Scotland spoke out with a more articulate and more insistent voice on temperance." At this Assembly also he made one of his first powerful speeches in connection with the Church Union movement. His work in connection with that movement is dealt with in a later chapter, but this speech made so great an impression that reference must be made to it at this stage because of its decisive effect on his future. It was declared to be " the " speech of the Assembly and it established his reputation. Dr. A. W. Fergusson, of Dundee, writing at the time in the *British Weekly* said—" The peroration to Dr. Wallace Williamson's speech was, by common consent, judged to be the most moving bit of eloquence in the whole ten days of the Assembly proceedings. The speech with most ' grip ' in it, however, was that of ' White of the Barony ' at the private Conference on the Monday night. On Tuesday he was good, but not so supremely good, in the general debate. These two speeches, along with his powerful appeals on the social work and for the temperance cause in our Church, marked him as the ' coming man,' if not already the ' man of the hour.' His admirers could claim, indeed, that this was ' White's Assembly.' "

The purely ecclesiastical side has by no means monopolised Dr. White's interests and activities. Temperance and other aspects of social reform, as proved by one of his early speeches just quoted, have strongly appealed to him. He has been almost as conspicuous as a social reformer as he has been as an ecclesiastic, and he has never ceased to plead for the necessity of the Church making itself a living force in the world to-day. In the Assembly of 1915 he moved the adoption of the report of the Christian Life and Work Committee in what was said to be a stirring and penetrating speech. Referring to the way in which Professor Charteris had overthrown "a mighty apathy " in the Church, and reviewing the details of the Committee's operations, he offered two constructive criticisms. Church services, he said, did not always lead to the service of the Church, and he appealed to members of the Guild to undertake systematic parochial work. Further, he said, the Church would regain its lost authority in religious thought only when it awoke to the fact that it could not claim the title to leadership in virtue of its office, but only in virtue of its capacity, when it could return to and retain that passionate zeal for righteousness and untiring zeal for spiritual service, which has been the characteristic of the early Reformed Church. There was a danger, he said, of the Christian Life and Work Committee being " subcommitteed " into feebleness, and he urged that more stress should be laid on Christian *Life* and less on Christian *Work*. This committee had been cradled in prayer and it must be upheld by prayer.

The Assembly of 1917 found him again speaking out strongly and with incisive eloquence on social questions in connection with the report of the Social Work Committee. He demanded that the Committee should go deeper into the social question than they were doing. They should consider what could be done to prevent social wreckage. The social work of the Church was not its work of charity ; it was to inculcate a keener sense of social justice which would make the other charity unnecessary. Many were social inefficients, not simply owing to moral causes, but to social and environmental mal-adjustments for which society had some responsibility. It was not to moral causes only that they owed their slums and gloomy alleys, " where progress halts on palsied feet." The sadness of the slum was that the denizens were willing occupants. The lack of goods for high wants was not so bad as the lack of want for the higher goods. Society had pressed their heart's desire out of them, and the Church had been impotent in face of their menacing problem. In politics the 'wait and see' policy had been condemned ; but a worse policy in moral questions was to ' see—and wait.' "

Later in the same Assembly he roused the members by a speech on the temperance question, pleading that it should not be regarded as one of mere intellectual interest—it was of vital and human interest. He quoted the saying of a Serbian statesman to the effect that " if Britain is defeated, she will be self-defeated," and in referring to those who argued that the by-products of liquor manufacture provided food for animals he remarked that they reminded him of the

American who burned the prairie to cook his breakfast.

The year 1918 marked the definite start of the Mission for National Re-dedication with which Dr. White was so prominently identified. At a crowded meeting of Assembly Dr. Wallace Williamson submitted the report of a Commission on the War in relation to its Spiritual, Moral and Social Issues. Dr. White followed Dr. Williamson with a powerful speech in which he declared that they needed a revival of national religious life that would shake them out of their ruts—for it was " rutualism " and not ritualism that was the enemy to-day. They needed deliverance from a bondage, silent and unrealised, the bondage of little hopes and ideals and thoughts which were begotten of unbelief in the omnipotence of God and an unreadiness to do His will. He found a telling illustration in Cavour's attitude to the unification of Italy. " Why not reform the Kingdom of Naples to begin with ? " Cavour was asked. " No," he replied. " No one will die for Naples, but thousands will die for Italy. Unify Italy and Naples will be reformed." A great aim like Natural Re-dedication—or better still—the Kingdom of God in this Kingdom of Scotland and in the Empire, he continued, would touch the imaginations of men with the vision of a world shaking itself free from its own blood-stained and tragic past. The opportunity was great, the Divine call clear. The success of the movement would depend on the grace of God and the blessing and work of the Holy Ghost, but there must be an atmosphere of faith, earnestness, prayer and expectation throughout the whole Church.

Dr. White was responsible for the preparation of the leaflet on " National Re-dedication ; a Brief Resume of Leading Points for Workers," which was so highly approved that copies were sent to every minister. In addition he was frequently called upon to address special meetings all over the country once the Mission had been generally taken up by the Synods throughout the Church. In the West of Scotland he did much to arouse a real interest in the movement and his influence was widely and deeply felt. One encouraging feature of the Mission was the cordial co-operation of the Churches. Church Union was not one of the objects aimed at but it was achieved in many districts in such a degree as to make it seem more than ever a practical proposition. In the rising spiritual temperature not a few differences and difficulties became less formidable in appearance. Dr. Wallace Williamson afterwards remarked that the movement had been abundantly successful all over the country, for, while it had not been in all parts all that they could have desired, it had done a great work in recalling to the minds of the people of Scotland her great historic national ideal—the fear of God.

Out of the mission, and as one of its results, there sprang the Church and Nation Committee of the General Assembly of which, at its inception in 1919, Dr. White was appointed Joint Convener along with Lord Sands. This position he has continued to hold until 1929, and many of his greatest speeches in the Assembly have been delivered in submitting the " Church and Nation" report. With the single exception of Church Union no other subject has so largely engaged his attention or so fully drawn out his powers.

Generally stated, the function of the Committee was to relate to " the duties of the Church in regard to the life of the Nation ; " while its task was more specifically defined as being to " watch over the developments of the Nation's life in which moral and spiritual considerations specially arise, and to consider what action the Church from time to time might be advised to take to further the interests of the people." The Assembly specially instructed the Committee to make enquiry regarding the desirability of definite action along such lines as (*a*) Training for the work of the Ministry, (*b*) Mobility in the Ministry, (*c*) Flexibility in Church Services, (*d*) Increase of the Democratic Element in Church Life, (*e*) The question of the position of women in the Church's work and counsels, (*f*) The question of how best to commend the teaching of Jesus Christ to those who are seeking to solve the problems of industrial life.

To these subjects many others were added from time to time, such as the Lambeth Proposals for the Re-union of Christendom, the question of Presbyterial Superintendence, the problem of

Irish Immigration, the proposed Amendment of the Education (Scotland) Act, 1918, in regard to Religious Instruction, to quote only a few. It was a very general commission, and Dr. White in submitting the Annual reports in the Assembly had always a wide field to cover. He had no easy task, but it was acknowledged that he handled his diverse themes with a mastery of detail and a vigour of diction which were at once arresting and impressive. Never perhaps did he show his statesmanlike grasp of affairs to better purpose than in his great " Church and Nation " speeches in the Assembly. It has sometimes been said that the wide scope of the Committee's work gives too big a subject for any man to deal with in one speech unless he has the real gift, the rare gift, of proportion and perspective. This, however, Dr. White has time and again shown he possesses in rare measure. He has never lost himself in a maze of details, or facts, or fancies ; he has kept "his feet firm planted all the time on mother earth, with the vision of the Christian statesman in his soul."

From year to year Dr. White had been steadily growing in power and influence in the Assembly and in the Church at large, and in the autumn of 1924 a movement was initiated by ministers and laymen in Glasgow and the West of Scotland to recognise his herculean labours in the cause of Church Union and in Church affairs generally. It was resolved that he should be entertained at a complimentary dinner, and this was held in

IN THE GENERAL ASSEMBLY

Glasgow on Friday, October 24, 1924. On that occasion a very representative company assembled in his honour, with the Moderator of the Synod of Glasgow and Ayr presiding, and in reply to the toast of the evening Dr. White delivered an important address on the progress and prospects of the Union negotiations. It was a signal honour enthusiastically paid by those who knew him best, and it attracted attention throughout the country.

A month later there came the crowning honour of his career in his nomination for the Moderatorship of the General Assembly. That he would eventually be called to this office had been regarded on all hands as not only probable but practically inevitable, and there was widespread satisfaction that the call had come while he was still in the fulness of his strength and the plentitude of his powers.

In his own Presbytery, Dr. White was not only the acknowledged leader but also one of the most faithful members. Growing fame and wider interests never led to any slackening in his Presbytery work, and his fellow Presbyters in Glasgow were among the first to congratulate him on his nomination for the Chair of the General Assembly. He was entertained by them and presented with an address in the following terms :

"We, your co-presbyters, are met here to-night and have asked you to be present in order that we may congratulate you on the honour for which you have been designated, and say how cordially we recognise the wisdom of that choice. We recall that you began your ministry among us on your ordination to the parish of Shettleston. There it fell to you to see that a suitable church was provided in room of the old church which was no longer habitable. It was a task calling for initiative and resolution ; the great church of Shettleston is lasting witness to the success which crowned your efforts. Thereafter you left us for the East, but in due time you returned to be minister of the Barony. In that great parish, which has so great traditions, and such a long line of distinguished ministers, you have justified the high expectations of those who called you, and have proved yourself a worthy successor of the great men who have preceded you. Especially are we grateful to you that, with all your heavy parochial duties and the claims which the social and philanthropic work of Glasgow have made upon you, you have yet taken your full share of Presbytery work. In the councils of the Church at large you hold an honoured place, and from the Church you have received many marks of confidence. And if the negotiations between the Assembly's Committee and the heritors resulted, as they did, in agreement upon the measure embodied in the Bill now before Parliament, it is in no small degree due to you that the terms are such as to have secured the unanimous endorsement and approval of the General Assembly. And soon you are to be Moderator of the Assembly, which means that there lies before you a strenuous and exacting year. That you will worthily fulfil the duties we have no manner of doubt ; and we pray that the goodness and mercy of God may follow you, not only in your Moderatorship, but all the days of your life."

At this time also there was a remarkable movement on the part of laymen throughout Scotland to make some tangible recognition of Dr. White's services. A representative committee was formed which included laymen of the Church of Scotland, the United Free Church, the Congregationalists, Baptists and others, with the result that a cheque for a handsome amount was sent him on the eve of his entry on the Moderatorship.

Other congratulations poured in upon Dr. White. It was not his own Church only that rejoiced in his appointment ; there was a general chorus of approval from all other denominations in the land. And not only so, but many people both high and low, who are not usually interested in the selection of Moderators, took the opportunity publicly and privately of conveying their congratulations. It was a proof—if proof were needed—that Dr. White was more than an ecclesiastic ; that he had become one of the leading public figures of the day, a man in whom the people, irrespective of Church connection, were keenly interested and of whom as a great Scotsman they felt they had reason to be proud.

When the late Dr. G. H. Morrison visited the

Assembly in 1926 as Moderator of the United Free Church he amused the House by telling of a meeting he had with Dr. White in a Glasgow street. It had been some years previously, and Dr. Morrison had expressed the hope that Dr. White would soon be Moderator. "Putting his hand on my shoulder," continued Dr. Morrison, " and looking earnestly in my face (for when he likes Dr. White can look very earnest !) he said ' Morrison, don't wish that, for once you are a Moderator you are dead and buried.' I'm not sure," added Dr. Morrison amid loud laughter, " that buried was the word he used but in any case he has been a false prophet for once."

In Dr. White's case the Moderatorship only led, as we shall see, to still further developments of his activity and influence.

CHAPTER XI

THE MODERATOR

WHEN Dr. White was installed in the Chair of the General Assembly of 1925, many prophecies were fulfilled. The earliest had been made thirty-one years previously by Principal Story at the Glasgow Elders' Assembly Dinner in Edinburgh. It was the first of these annual functions at which Dr. White was present and the Principal, on that evening in 1894, predicted that the young minister—who had been ordained only the previous year at Shettleston—would one day be Moderator of Assembly. It required less prescience on the part of those who had been associated with Dr. White after he came to take an active part in the work of the Assembly and other Church Courts, to realise that he was destined for the highest place. His ascendancy in the Assembly had become more pronounced with every passing year, and when he stepped into the Chair it was felt on all hands that the right man was in the right place.

But there was another reason for general satisfaction. It was known that the Assembly of 1925 would be one of historic significance, when decisions fraught with great issues regarding the

Church's tenure of her Property and Endowments would be recorded, and when a critical stage in the Church Union negotiations would be reached. " Accordingly," it was said, " the question of who would be Moderator in that fateful year became one of more than ordinary interest. When it became known that the name to be put forward was that of ' John White of the Barony,' the Church rested, knowing that it would be well and truly led, and that in great days a great man would preside over its councils."

It was the subject of common remark that Dr. White took to the Moderatorship as he had taken to the Assembly itself many years before as " to the manner born." For one thing he looked every inch the part in the Moderator's dress. With his commanding presence and wearing his official robes and hood, lace ruffles and glittering war medals, he made an impressive figure. His clear cut features, pale austere countenance and eagle profile, so impressed one distinguished critic that he thought he might have " served a painter for the imagined portrait of a Scottish mitred Abbot of the Pre-Reformation Church." Another, after watching him in the Moderator's Chair, declared that in the Church of Rome he could not have missed his Cardinal's Hat !

While he bore himself with a fine dignity befitting his high office, he revealed another aspect of his personality when it fell to him to deliver the courtesy speeches from the chair. Nothing could have been more gracious than the way in which he gave to these brief ceremonial addresses the kindly personal touch which made them linger long in the memory of those to whom they were addressed, whether visitors from other shores or servants of the Church called forward to receive recognition of their work.

As far as the actual conduct of the business of the Assembly was concerned, there never perhaps had been such a Moderator. Many other distinguished Moderators, conscious of their own limitations in regard to business procedure, had largely left the guidance of affairs in the hands of the officials at the Table. Not so Dr. White. He required no assistance and no promptings. He was equal to dealing with every emergency himself. It was quite apparent he was in his native element, and he ruled with a sure, firm hand which the Assembly quickly appreciated and to which it readily responded. Writing at the time an experienced and acute observer said—" He is the Moderator born. Such grip, such ease, such swiftness, we have seldom if ever seen. Standing Orders are his vital breath. His rulings from the Chair come with a kind of cosmic inevitableness, like Nature's very own ; Assembly members could as soon think of appealing against the sunrise or the Tweed ! "

The outstanding event of this Assembly was the presentation by Dr. White of the Report of the Special Committee appointed to deal with the legislation on the Property and Endowments of the Church. In order to present this report he left the Chair and, divested of his gown, took his place on the floor of the Assembly to make what was declared to be, up till then, the greatest speech of his career.

It was, indeed, a memorable scene. The Assembly Hall was densely crowded, the packed public galleries testifying to the wide general interest, and there were several distinguished visitors. The venerable leader of the United Free Church, Dr. Archibald Henderson, was accommodated on a front bench where he could more easily follow the proceedings ; two Ex-Moderators of that Church, Dr. Drummond and Dr. Inch, sat in the throne gallery beside Mrs. White, while many men prominent in the public life of Scotland outside ecclesiastical circles were present to follow proceedings which they recognised would mean so much for the future of their country.

It was a tense atmosphere, and when Dr. White rose at the call of the Acting Moderator, " at the same instant the Assembly rose as one man in his honour like an Army ready for the word of command from its leader." The House of Lords having the previous night passed the Property and Endowments Bill, Dr. White declared that in that Bill they had done what they could for the unifying of Scottish Presbyterianism, and he was confident their friends of the United Free Church would not fail to respond to their approach. Having explained the position in detail he concluded a great and moving speech with a noble peroration in an appeal for deeper spirituality in the Church which at the close brought the members once more to their feet. Dr. White had a third ovation from an upstanding Assembly when Dr. Cathels from the Chair expressed their " profound admiration for the power with which he had stated the case and for the tremendous service he had rendered to the Church at that time."

Dr. Archibald Henderson afterwards wrote Dr. White :

" May I take the liberty of thanking you for your speech which, as I was close to you, I heard. If we could all keep, or be kept rather, on the same zealous and loyal devotion, all the great mountains some see—or think they see— before us would become a plain. I trust you will be given health and vigour of mind and body to see that plain. Whatever occur to cause a halt—I pray nothing will—do not let go your full assurance of the sincere and devoted purpose of the brethren of the United Free Church to see this through for the blessing of Scotland and the honour of our common Lord."

Dr. White devoted his closing address to the subject of " Efficiency "—a characteristic subject as Professor W. P. Paterson afterwards described it. It was a statesmanlike survey of the whole situation and a clarion call to unity and consecration in the work of the Church. " An utterance worthy of a great and memorable Assembly," was the description of it given by an eminent Church leader. And the Lord High Commissioner, the Earl of Elgin, in his address from the Throne made the following special reference : " In that masterly, eloquent and stirring address so full of courage, prudence and wisdom with which you have concluded the deliberations of the Assembly, you have sounded a clear call to duty and to service."

The Earl of Elgin had proved himself one of the most popular in a long line of Lord High Commissioners, and his relations with Dr. White as Moderator had been particularly friendly. In a closing acknowledgment His Grace made the following personal allusion : " These thanks of mine would indeed be incomplete, Right Reverend Moderator, were I not to express the feelings of respect, admiration and esteem with which I regard yourself. I admire and respect your ability as Chairman, but I esteem and value the personal friendship you have given me. If this Assembly has opened its arms in welcome, you have opened your heart, and the smile with which you greeted me each morning was like the burst of sunshine on a cloudy day."

While Dr. White had been distinguishing himself in the Moderator's Chair, Mrs. White had been exercising a peculiarly gracious influence of her own. As the wife of the Moderator she had a place in the Throne Gallery, and it was a greatly prized honour to be asked to accompany her there. She sought to share this privilege

Photo : Lafayette]   [Glasgow

THE MODERATOR AND MRS. WHITE

with as many ladies of the manse as possible, not restricting it to her own personal friends, but making a point of inviting for each day, say the wife of a convener who would be submitting a report, or the wife of some member who was expected to address the Assembly. Her anxious solicitude that no one should be overlooked won the hearts of all who were familiar with what was going on behind the scenes.

Among others who enjoyed the privilege of a seat beside Mrs. White one day in the Throne Gallery was Miss Ishbel MacDonald, daughter of Mr. Ramsay MacDonald, the Labour Prime Minister. The invitation to his daughter was highly appreciated by Mr. Ramsay MacDonald, who wrote that he would very much like that she should see the Assembly in session while she was in Edinburgh.

During the Assembly period Dr. and Mrs. White gave three " At Homes " in the Freemasons Hall, Edinburgh, and seldom have there been such representative and distinguished gatherings of the kind. As Dr. White explained, the idea was to give the members of Assembly and other friends an opportunity of meeting some of those who had taken a prominent part in the legislation in connection with the Church Union negotiations. This object was very happily attained. Among those who not only attended but also addressed the guests were Viscount Haldane, the former Lord Chancellor ; Viscount Novar, the Duke of Buccleuch (who came specially to Edinburgh for the purpose) and Sir John Gilmour, Bart., Secretary of State for Scotland, all of whom had done much in various ways in connection with the Church Bills. The presence of Viscount Haldane was specially appreciated, as he had come immediately after the funeral of his mother, which Dr. White had attended along with his chaplains. It had been his mother's wish, said Lord Haldane, that he should come to that gathering and he knew could she have foreseen the circumstances in which he was to be there, she would still have desired it. He made an important speech on the Church Bill and, referring to Dr. White, said—" We seem at last to be nearing the end of a long road in this great movement, and I am very glad that you, as the leader, are Moderator."

Among others prominent in the negotiations who had hoped to be present but were unavoidably absent were the Lord Advocate, the Hon. William Watson, K.C., M.P., and Mr H. P. MacMillan, K.C., both of whom had been intimately associated with the legislation. Leading representatives—both clerical and lay—attended from the United Free Church, and the genial ex-Moderator, Dr. A. S. Inch of Dumbarton, enlivened the proceedings with one of his characteristic stories. It was of a young couple in Glasgow who were keeping company and had two weekly engage-ments—one at the Church on Sunday evening and the other at Hope Street on Thursday evening. On parting one Sunday, the young man said to his sweetheart, "It will be Hope Street on Thursday," and she replied, "Don't you think we might try Union Street for a change?" Their Churches, Dr. Inch added amid great applause, had been in Hope Street long enough, but they were going to be in Union Street soon.

At a dinner given in Edinburgh, at the close of the Assembly, Dr. White as Moderator had around him a most distinguished and representative company. On the Moderator's right were Dr. James Harvey, Moderator of the United Free Church, Mr. J. A. S. Millar, W.S., and Principal Martin, and on his left Lord Sands, Dr. R. J. Drummond and Mr. William Whitelaw. Among others present were Dr. Cathels, Dr. John Smith, Dr. J. N. Ogilvie, Dr. Paul, Dr. McClymont, Dr. Thomas Martin, Dr. Norman Maclean, Lord Constable, Lord Murray, Sheriff Orr, Dr. A. N. Bogle, the Rev. William White and the Moderator's Chaplains, the Rev. J. McNeill Frazer and the Rev. R. H. Kerr.

Among the congratulations which reached Dr. White on the successful completion of a memorable Moderatorship of the Assembly were messages from all classes, clerical and lay, rich and poor, from men and women of title and from humble folk whose names have never been in print. Not a few were from those in other Churches than his own, and one of the most striking was from Professor James Stalker, D.D., formerly of Aberdeen United Free Church College, who had just returned from a holiday in Italy and had gone to spend the years of his retirement at Crieff.   Professor Stalker wrote :

"*June* 15, 1925.

" DEAR DR. WHITE,

" It was beside the blue waters of the Lake of Como that I read with edification and delight your two great deliverances to the General Assembly, and I write to express the desire, which, I am sure, many will share, that they may be made accessible in a more permanent form—the one most important as a portion of Scottish history and the other inspirational in the highest degree.

" It seemed to me, perusing the reports daily in the newspapers, that the personality of the Moderator on this occasion dominated the scene to an unusual extent, and this was all to the good. I congratulate you on thus being able to leave your mark on a critical year.

" My only doubt about your Moderatorship was whether you should not have been reserved for the actual year of Union.   We are all hoping that our Grand Old Man—beside whom I have just come to live—may be spared to see the great event—but, even if this were so, he would require a colleague in the Moderatorial Chair, and for this office I can think of none so suitable as yourself.

" Yours most truly,
" (*Signed*) JAMES STALKER."

The first engagement Dr. White fulfilled after

the closing of the Assembly was in Edinburgh on the following day, when he was the guest of the Town Council on the occasion of the presentation in the Usher Hall of the freedom of the City to Mr. Ramsay MacDonald. At the luncheon in the City Chambers after the ceremony he proposed the toast of the Lord Provost in a racy and eloquent speech.

Engrossed as he was with the work of many committees, Dr. White at once threw himself whole-heartedly into the visitation of the Churches in outlying districts which has now become a recognised part of the Moderator's duties. In addition to fulfilling many separate engagements in other parts of the country he entered on a tour of the congregations in the Highlands and Islands. Beginning in the County of Ross, his attention was next given to Sutherland, and after visiting the parishes that fringe the North Sea, he crossed to the West to overtake those on the Atlantic Coast. A visit to Iona, where he preached in the Cathedral, was followed by a few days of rest before he set out, accompanied by Dr. Macfarlane, Kingussie, on another Apostolic journey covering the far flung Synod of Glenelg, which includes the Hebrides and much of the mainland, with thirteen parishes and five mission stations from Mallaig to Loch Broom. A weekend was spent in the romantic parish of small isles in the Presbytery of Skye—the islands of Eigg, Rhum, Canna and Muck. No Moderator had ever before been able to set foot on these small islands owing to the difficulty of communication. The parish minister and the parish doctor of the four islands, however, now share a small open motor boat for their respective parochial duties which they carry out simultaneously; and in their company the Moderator, in full Court dress, negotiated difficult landings on rocky shores and was received by the people with enthusiasm. When he had landed on the mainland at Mallaig, he had sailed one hundred miles in this modern " coracle." Himself no mean sailor, he did most of the steering and he " encountered darkness and fog as his predecessor, St. Columba, had done long before."

From the farthest Hebrides he hastened to an entirely different environment in response to a command to preach before the King and Queen in the Church at Crathie and to be the guest of Their Majesties at Balmoral Castle for the week-end. He was summoned in a two-fold capacity—not only as Moderator of the General Assembly of the Church of Scotland (who usually receives a command during his year of office to preach before the King), but also as one of His Majesty's Chaplains in Scotland. That Dr. White embraced the opportunity of keeping Their Majesties informed of the ecclesiastical situation in Scotland is apparent from the sermon he preached before them at Crathie. To Royalty as to the common people he enlarged on the importance and necessity of the Union of the Churches. In view of the special circumstances a brief epitome of this sermon may be of interest.

He chose for his text Isaiah 62, 1, 6, 7, " For Zion's sake will I not hold my peace———." It had been a great privilege, he said, to visit the Churches in outlying places in Ross and Cromarty and Sutherland, in Iona and in the Western Isles ; to see there the watchmen upon the walls who held not their peace day nor night, who made mention of the Lord and kept not silence ; and to speak in the name of the Church a word of encouragement to the King's remembrancers that they give the Lord no rest until He made the Church within our land a praise in the earth. At last General Assembly it was a strong conviction behind all their deliberations that 1925 was an epoch-making year in their Scottish Church history ; that God was decreeing some new and great period in their Church ; and that the highest Church policy consisted in discovering, so far as might be, the direction in which God was moving in their midst, and in clearing away all obstacles to His progress. Face to face with that changing order, it was their duty to ask if the Church was adapting itself to meet the new day and the new needs.

To be content with a place in the rearguard, contributing some little incidental benefit, was to fail in the primary purpose for which the Lord planted His Church in Scotland. The Church would meet the new day and fulfil the great purposes for which God had placed it in their beloved land, permeating and disciplining the coming social order by a spirit of Christian idealism, when there took place such a spiritual quickening in the membership of the Church as would lead to a higher standard of Christian living, a deepened sense of responsibility and a renewed zeal for His service.

A first great need to-day was a vital personal religion. If the Church was to be an effective spiritual force it must manifest its unity. Important as reunion was, something more was needed, without which the most perfect ecclesiastical machinery would be ineffective and a mere turning of wheels. The Holy Spirit was the dynamic of the Church in all its endeavours to bring the world to Christ.

Some weeks later Dr. White accompanied the King and Queen when they visited Aberdeen to open the Cowdray Hall and Art Museum, and on that occasion, along with Dr. Harvey, Moderator of the United Free Church, and Principal Sir George Adam Smith, he dedicated the Aberdeen War Memorial.

The next Moderatorial tour undertaken was in the Synod of Angus and Mearns (including the city of Dundee), where, in the later months of the year, Dr. White completed the work begun by his predecessor Dr. Cathels. In April, 1926, he visited the Presbyteries of Lochmaben and Dumfries, and, as was the case in his Northern tour, he visited practically every rural parish in the area as well as many of the urban parishes,

THE MODERATOR

When engaged in these Moderatorial tours, Dr. White met everywhere with a very cordial welcome. Many public receptions were held in his honour—Dundee for example gave him a civic reception—and in not a few instances the Churches of other denominations held united services on the occasion of his visit. He never spared himself, but found time amid his numerous engagements to perform many a kindly act of courtesy to obscure servants of the Church in out-of-the-way places. Hearing in an isolated parish of a venerable elder who was unable on account of old age to attend the public meeting, he would pay him a Moderatorial visit in his own humble home, or he would slip off quietly to call on some ailing parishioners and give these people, far removed from the centre of things, the assurance that their Church was not indifferent to them. Before he left Dundee he mixed freely with the farmers in their weekly market at the foot of Crichton Street, where it was remarked that the pomp and circumstance denoted by his official raiment did not overshadow his genial person-ality. " Everyone," it was said, " was interested in his ' two-handed crack ' with an old farmer just before he entered the motor car which was to convey him to Broughty Ferry."

There were amusing incidents and experiences on these tours, and no one enjoyed the humour of them more than Dr. White himself. The official Moderatorial dress was, naturally, a puzzle to many who had never before come into contact with a Moderator. At one of the receptions given in his honour a young lady remarked to her friend, " Isn't the Moderator a dear with his ruffles ? " " Oh," said the other, " I haven't seen him. Has he come yet ? " " Why," was the staggering reply, " you shook hands with him as you entered." " Him ? " gasped the ignorant one. " Is he the Moderator ? I thought he was a footman ! "

A little girl in Sutherlandshire asked special permission of her parents to stay up late as she wanted to see the " Radiator " and Dr. White afterwards remarked that he was proud of that name, for he felt that Scotland was greatly in need of central heating. In a Forfar manse, one of the children persisted in calling him the " Modulator " and he was glad of that description also, since a " modulator " was connected with harmony and rhythm, and he had been going through the length and breadth of Scotland seeking to introduce rhythm and harmony among the Churches.

In addition to the Moderatorial tours arranged by the Assembly's Committee he undertook many other engagements in all parts of the country, his time being fully occupied throughout the whole of his year of office. One interesting event in which he took a leading part was the commemoration of the centenary of John Macleod Campbell, of Row, the theologian around whose teaching so great a controversy had raged in the Church in the early part of the nineteenth century. Another was when he took part, along with Earl Haig and Earl Jellicoe, in the Remembrance Day celebrations at the Mercat Cross in Edinburgh and afterwards preached the sermon at the service in St. Giles Cathedral.

In October Dr. and Mrs. White gave a reception in the McLellan Galleries, Glasgow, at which there was a large attendance, representative of practically all the denominations in the City. Among the speakers who offered congratulations were Principal Sir Donald MacAlister of Glasgow University; the Bishop of Glasgow and Galloway ; the Moderator of Glasgow Presbytery ; the Rev. Dr. George H. Morrison of Wellington United Free Church, who spoke both as a former fellow student and a ministerial neighbour ; the Very Rev. Professor Milligan ; Sir John M. Macleod ; and Colonel J. A. Roxburgh of the Glasgow United Free Church Office-Bearers' Association.

When the time came for Dr. White to lay down the office of Moderator, the country was in the throes of the General Strike, and the General Assembly of 1926 met merely to adjourn for another fortnight. But before it adjourned, Dr. White had passed from one great office to another. He left the Moderator's Chair only to take his place at the head of the Table as Convener of the Business Committee, and " leader of the House," a position to which he was called by common consent and for which his whole life and training had been one continuous preparation. From that time onwards he became the nominal as well as actual " leader," with an unchallenged authority such as has rarely been witnessed in all the years of the Assembly.

CHAPTER XII

CHURCH UNION

THIS volume is not meant to serve as a history of the Church Union movement and it would be impossible, even if it were desirable, within the compass of such a work to trace the whole story of the negotiations or to deal in detail with all the aspects of the question. Since, however, it has been in connection with the cause of Church Union in Scotland that Dr. White has risen to the full height of his powers, and has come most prominently before the world at large, it is necessary to pass some of the main events in a brief and rapid survey in order to trace his intimate association with every stage of the movement.

It may be explained for the benefit of readers outside Scotland, and unfamiliar with the circumstances, that there were two great Presbyterian denominations living and working side by side, the ancient Church of Scotland itself and the United Free Church composed of sections which had left the Church of Scotland at the Secession and Disruption in former generations. These two main streams in the ecclesiastical life of Scotland had been gradually flowing closer together until many came to cherish the dream that one day they would be merged in one. Twenty years ago the first steps were taken to secure the realisation of that dream, but only now is it within prospect of fulfilment.

Long before Dr. White came to his present position as the acknowledged leader in the Union movement he had been " the power behind the throne," and in every development of the protracted negotiations he had taken an active and influential part. It is even the case, although the fact may not be generally known, that he took an important share in the initiation of the earliest steps in the movement, and his action on that occasion even affected the whole subsequent course of affairs. To-day he is one of the few survivors of the original band of men who set in motion the forces which are only now coming to full fruition.

It is well known that the first motion on the subject was submitted to the Church of Scotland General Assembly in 1907. Previous to that, however, there had been private and informal meetings of members of the Church of Scotland and the United Free Church, Dr. William Mair, of Earlston, taking a prominent part in connection with these from the Church of Scotland side. Mr. White, then the young minister of South Leith, was invited to attend. He happened to meet Dr. Archibald Scott in Edinburgh at the corner of Frederick Street and George Street and mentioned the matter to him. Dr. Scott was then the "leader" of the Church of Scotland Assembly, and the foremost influence in its affairs, but he had not been invited to these private meetings. He advised Mr. White to keep clear and said he would raise the matter by overture in the Presbytery of Edinburgh with the view of placing the movement on open and official lines.

At the next meeting of Presbytery Dr. Scott introduced an overture proposing *co-operation* with the United Free Church. The overture received general support and was spoken to by Dr. Scott, Dr. Cameron Lees, and Professor W. P. Paterson. Mr. White asked Dr. Scott to widen the overture to include an invitation to other churches and in particular the Free Church of Scotland. His chief contention, however, was that the invitation should not be to co-operate but to unite. At this stage the only support he received was from the Rev. James Park, of St. John's Parish, Leith.

In the evening of that day, however, after the Presbytery meeting, Dr. Scott telephoned to Mr. White at South Leith Manse with a request that he would meet him in the Church Offices, 22, Queen Street, Edinburgh, next morning. When they met, Dr. Scott at once remarked to Mr. White, " You are right with regard to the invitation being extended to the Free Church at least, but I cannot go beyond co-operation." At the next meeting of Presbytery, Dr. Scott withdrew his former overture and submitted one on these lines. What seemed to be a general impression regarding this change of attitude was expressed by Dr. Forrest, of West Coates, when he remarked—" White has won."

DR. JOHN WHITE

In the 1908 General Assembly the question came up on Friday, May 22, when Dr. Norman Macleod moved the motion on the lines of Dr. Scott's overture recommending a conference on co-operation but proposing certain restrictions, and Professor W. P. Paterson seconded. The Rev. Alfred Warr, of Rosneath, moved a direct negative but was defeated by an overwhelming majority. A further motion was submitted by Mr. White recommending a conference, but for the definite purpose of discovering the difficulties which stood in the way of reunion. His motion, though well supported, failed to carry, but it made a very distinct impression on the Assembly. The *Scottish Review* declared it was " the best motion in the circumstances," and this was borne out by subsequent events.

In the following week the United Free Church Assembly, still in session, also discussed the question. On Wednesday, May 27, 1908, its venerable leader, Dr. Archibald Henderson, moved a motion reconsidering the terms of the Church of Scotland's approach, setting down the Church's position and remitting the matter to a large and representative committee. The finding was against co-operation, and favoured unrestricted conference on Union. In conversation with Mr. White immediately thereafter, Dr. Henderson said he had moved in his Assembly against co-operation for reasons very similar to those which Mr. White had submitted in the Church of Scotland Assembly. Thus began an intimate friendship between the two men who, perhaps, more than any other in their respective Churches, influenced the whole course of the Union movement. In the following year the negotiations for Union were definitely opened.

The General Assembly on May 27, 1909, declared the readiness of the Church of Scotland to enter into unrestricted conference with their brethren of the United Free Church on the existing ecclesiastical situation, and on the main causes which keep the Churches apart, in the earnest hope that, by God's blessing, misunderstandings and hindrances might be removed, and the great object of Presbyterian re-union in Scotland thereby advanced. It was agreed that a committee of Ministers and Elders should be appointed to represent the Church in conference with representatives of the United Free Church. Dr. Norman Macleod and Lord Balfour of Burleigh were elected joint-conveners, and the Rev. John White, of South Leith, Secretary of the Committee. Thus began Dr. White's connection with the movement, which has continued uninterruptedly until its final consummation.

From the very first he made his influence felt in the committee. No one was so intimately familiar with every aspect of the situation or had a mind readier to grasp and deal with the various points as they arose. He was consulted on all important matters by every leader in the movement. Dr. Archibald Scott's conversations with him at the very start of the Movement have already been mentioned. And Dr. William Mair, of Earlston, whose name also must always be associated with the origin of the negotiations, sought his opinion on many of the difficulties, and to the close of his life maintained a correspondence on the subject. Lord Balfour of Burleigh, that sane and sagacious churchman, the foremost layman of the Church of Scotland of his day, who led the Union movement until his death, came to rely more and more on the judgment, the skill and the constructive ability of the Secretary of the Committee. He lost no opportunity of taking counsel with him, personally or by correspondence, concerning every important move in the negotiations.

When Lord Balfour's joint convener, Dr. Norman Macleod, passed away and Dr. Wallace Williamson was appointed his successor, Dr. White's authority and influence in the Committee became still more pronounced. Lord Sands in his biography of Dr. Wallace Williamson has said that Dr. Williamson's " service to Church Union was inspirational rather than constructive ; he was receptive rather than suggestive. In private conference and negotiation he was cautious and reticent. He took everything in, but he preferred to leave it to those in whom he had confidence to advance propositions and to meet objections." This gave all the greater opportunity for the display of original genius and constructive power on the part of Dr. White, and there devolved on him more and more the direction of affairs in the Union Committee even while he was still only its Secretary. When Dr. Williamson's health gave way in 1924, Dr. White succeeded him as Joint-Convener and became the titular as well as the actual leader.

Of Dr. White's incessant labours in the Union Committee and of his undaunted courage and optimism in face of difficulties which were apt to dismay even the strongest, only those who were in some way associated with him have any adequate idea. Long before he became Joint Convener he made speeches of first rate importance on the subject in the General Assembly. As early as 1914 he opened the Union discussion in what *The Scotsman* described as " a speech of great ability." " Mr. White," the report continued, " has rendered great service to the cause as Secretary to the Union Committee, and the cheers which greeted him showed how the Church has learned to trust and rely upon him. . . . In Mr. White the Assembly recognised a leader who is destined to wield a great influence on the councils of the Church. The great cause ever provides a leader."

But it was not alone by such great public appearances—of which this is but one example—that he was giving notable service to the cause. Much of his work was done behind the scenes, preparing the way for the committee's deliberations and actions. The secretaryship of the Committee was no sinecure yet time and again he added considerably to his labours. In 1913 the Committee thought it might be useful to place in the hands of members and officebearers of the Church a summary of the past proceedings, with excerpts from the more important Reports and Documents which had been submitted to the General Assembly since the Conferences began. This summary, not a bald statement but a pamphlet of forty-five pages, was compiled by Dr. White, and as a concise and comprehensive statement of the course of proceedings to that date it is now of historic value. That was only one of many instances of how additional duties were readily undertaken in order to serve the cause.

As an example of his constant watchfulness over everything which might in any way affect the cause of Union, and of his summing up of the position at this stage, there may be cited the correspondence which he had with Mr. Keir Hardie, M.P., the well known Labour leader. Speaking in the House of Commons in April, 1914, on the Welsh Church Bill, Mr. Keir Hardie made a reference to the Union negotiations which drew from Dr. White a letter explaining in detail the whole position of the movement.

" DEAR MR. KEIR HARDIE,
" In a report of your speech on the Welsh Church Bill which appeared in the *Glasgow Herald* on Tuesday, the 21st, there occur words which are somewhat vague and might mislead : ' Negotiations had been going on to unite the

whole Presbyterian Church in Scotland. There were earnest men in the United Free Church and the Established Church zealously working for union. The commission which had been sitting found that there was substantial agreement on ninety-nine points out of one hundred, but the stumbling block was Establishment. So long as that continued in Scotland, there would be no unity. A movement was forming itself in the minds of the leaders of the Churches in Scotland to once more reopen the whole question, not with the view of perpetuating sectarian differences, but to remove the last barrier which stood between the Churches of Scotland and their unification."

" Since 1909 the question of reunion has been before the Churches, and an earnest endeavour is being made to remove misunderstandings and hindrances, and to advance the great object of Presbyterian reunion in Scotland. Both Churches recognise that the present social and religious state of affairs at home, the pressing problems brought before the Church by democracy and science—the two great master forces of the age—and the great problem of evangelising the non-Christian peoples, render manifest the need for the reunion of our Scottish Presbyterianism. But the way to this reunion is not by way of disestablishment—it would be hopeless to seek it in this way. The proposal is to embody in what would be the constitution of the reunited Church, a declaration of Spiritual Freedom that would cover all matters spiritual ; this would be a practical satisfaction of the conception of Spiritual Freedom entertained by the United Free Church, and would be quite compatible with the historic position of the Church of Scotland. The term 'Establishment' is a very indefinite term, and has a very different significance in England from what it bears in Scotland—and in both countries it describes a different concordat between Church and State from what obtains on the Continent. The Committee of the Church of Scotland contend that (I quote from Report to General Assembly 1911), 'if the Church were declared to be in such a position of liberty from the authority of the State in matters spiritual as would satisfy the views of the United Free Church, and all enactments inconsistent therewith were repealed, the State recognition which they value would be adequately secured by the Treaty of Union and the Act of Security and other Statues therein adopted or ratified, in so far as not thus repealed, and by the continuance of the consuetudinary recognition by the Crown and its servants of the Church of Scotland as the national Church.'

" May I add one quotation from the Report to the General Assembly 1913—' The historical position of the Church as the national and representative Church, recognised by the State as such, and the usages which have gathered round that recognition, would not be prejudiced by the changes which are proposed. Whilst it is not proposed to define or reinforce this recognition by any new enactment, the Church of Scotland could not assent to any proposal which either required or implied its withdrawal.'

" Any true scheme of union must conserve the vital principles and traditions of both Churches. It would be a disaster to Church life and thought to seek union at the expense of the truth and principles which past divisions have brought into the full possession of the Church. Any true policy of union must be constructive, recognising what has been achieved through differentiation, and looking forward to a higher integration in which a place will be found for the gains of the past. The United Church of the future must embrace all that the Spirit has brought to pass in both branches of the Church. There are many of us who look hopefully for an ecclesiastical settlement in Scotland that will lay to rest all cries of Disestablishment and the counter cries of Establishment—so frequently without meaning on the lips of those who utter them. The duty of the hour requires us to go forward, not backward to the old divisions and the old battle-cries.

" May I add that as early as 1910 in our conferences with the United Free Church, there was general agreement as to the abiding obligation that lies upon the State not only to render practical obedience to the will of Christ in matters of policy, legislation, etc., but to take account of the Church of Christ also, to acknowledge the several branches thereof as institutions founded on faith and conscience, and responsible in things spiritual to Christ alone, and to further the interests of the Kingdom of God in all appropriate ways.

" Nothing that is proposed in the policy of reunion would prejudice the position of other Churches with whom corporate union is not at present practicable. The Church of Scotland would heartily sympathise with any proposals for legislation which would give these Churches an improved status in the eye of the law, and such proposals have already been outlined in the Memorandum of 1912. It has to be borne in mind, however, that the present legal status of these Churches as voluntary associations in the eye of the law does not differ from the legal status of all Churches in the colonies in which there is no State-recognised Church, and accordingly the disabilities under which the Churches labour do not flow from the State recognition accorded to the Church of Scotland, the disestablishment of which would simply extend the area of disability without any advantage in this respect to the other Churches.

" The one great question before us in Scotland is not what will place the one Church or the other in a better position as ecclesiastical institutions, but what will place the Church of Christ within the realm in a position of renewed strength and revived zeal to cope with the new forces—some aggressively non-Christian, others awaiting a spiritual baptism—that have sprung up in our midst within these last few decades. I am confident that in this earnest effort to reach a worthy ecclesiastical settlement in Scotland, we may rely on the active sympathy and intelligent support of our public men irrespective of party.

"   I remain,
"   Yours very sincerely,
"   (*Signed*) JOHN WHITE.

" P S.—I am forwarding to you an Explanatory Statement which, as Secretary to the Church of Scotland Committee, I had the duty of drawing up."

To that letter Mr. Keir Hardie replied as follows :

"   10 Nevill's Court,
"   London, E.C.,
                April 24, 1914.

" REVEREND AND DEAR SIR,

" I am greatly obliged by your interesting letter of 22nd current.   You will of course understand that what I said in the House of Commons in the speech to which you refer was not intended to cast any reflection upon the Church of Scotland, but only as an argument showing the difficulties which the Establishment may create when Union is being sought.   The subject of Scottish Union happened to be fresh in my mind, as only the day previous I spent some time in the company of one of the workers for unity from the U.F. side, who takes a very broad and tolerant view of the whole question and is not at all bigoted against the Establishment, but, to use his own words, the Commission which is seeking to unify the Churches finds itself up against ' a brick wall ' which the present form of Establishment creates. I sincerely trust the efforts of those who are working for the Union of the Churches in Scotland may be crowned with a speedy success.

"Yours faithfully,

"(*Signed*) J. KEIR HARDIE."

When the time came for an approach being made to Parliament for the necessary legislature, Dr. White proved invaluable to the Committee. In the General Assembly of 1920 Dr. Wallace Williamson, reporting on the negotiations with the Government, took the opportunity of making a warm acknowledgment of the services rendered by Dr. White in that way. One of his interesting experiences in this connection—and one of the earliest of his many Parliamentary interviews—was when, early in 1921, he went to London along with Dr. Wallace Williamson, Dr. Thomas Martin (then Moderator of Assembly), Lord Balfour of Burleigh, Lord Sands, and Mr. Alan L. Menzies, W.S., Agent of the Church, to interview the Prime Minister, Mr. Lloyd George. The interview took place in the historic Cabinet Room at 10, Downing Street, and the Prime Minister was accompanied by Mr. Bonar Law, Earl Balfour, better known as "A. J. B.," Mr. Robert Munro, Secretary for Scotland, and Sir Robert Horne.

In some impressions given later of this

memorable interview Dr. White said, " A. J. B."
was " the cleverest intellect and took his points
quickly," Bonar Law was " hardly less quick
in the practical difficulties," Munro was " the
alert lawyer." " It was," said Dr. White, " a
long road to travel for such a brief interview, but
it was momentous while it lasted. Very little
was said at the Table, but I gather that the Government will do something at once. It might
have a place in the King's speech, but there was
a disinclination to agree to commit themselves
to this by Bonar Law. My impression is that
the Government will introduce the Bill."

Dr. White's forecast was fulfilled. Before the
Assembly met in 1921, Mr. Bonar Law announced
in the House of Commons that the Government
proposed to introduce the desired Bill, and it was
passed through Parliament and became law in
July of that year.

By the Church of Scotland Act (1921), recognition was given to the rights, powers and liberties of
the Church as set forth in the Articles declaring
its constitution in matters spiritual, and it removed
a main cause of separation between the Churches.
It was recognised, however, at the passing of
the Act that the adoption of the Articles by the
Church of Scotland would render a change necessary regarding the tenure of the endowments.
Then followed a period of negotiation with the
Government, the heritors, and other parties
concerned which brought into play more than
ever the diplomatic skill, the legal knowledge and

the apparently inexhaustible resourcefulness of Dr. White, who was appointed joint convener of a special Committee to deal with the matter. No detail was too trivial for his attention and no difficulty too great for him to face. For months on end he practically lived at Westminster, sitting through the proceedings in the committee rooms at a convenient desk behind the bar ; watching the debates in the House of Commons from a seat under the gallery where also he was easily accessible for consultation ; and all the while missing no opportunity of interviewing Members of Parliament in the lobbies, enlightening them on the points at issue and bringing his personal influence to bear.

In submitting the report at the Assembly of 1924, Dr. White was in the happy position of being able to announce that, after anxious and lengthy negotiations, agreement had been reached with the heritors, an event so decisive of the fate of the Property and Endowments Bill that the Lord Advocate was moved to say " within these few minutes history has been made in Scotland." It was so great a moment in the Assembly that the business was interrupted while the Moderator offered a prayer of thanksgiving for the opening up thus far of the way to Union.

The Church of Scotland (Property and Endowments) Bill was under the charge of three different Governments in turn. It had been first introduced by a Unionist Government in January, 1924, and subsequently it was carried through the House of Lords by a Labour Government in July and read for a first time in the House of Commons. Then another Unionist Government had reintroduced it in the House of Commons, and it was hoped it would proceed without difficulty or delay through the House of Lords in time to become an Act of Parliament before the General Assembly, which would be in session in Edinburgh in May, 1925, had concluded its sittings. This, it was recognised, was of the utmost importance, so that the Church of Scotland should know before its Supreme Court adjourned for the year that the way was clear for proceeding towards Union. Almost at the last moment this seemed to become impossible.

After the Assembly was in session, intimation was received that, as the House of Lords did not sit on Mondays, there would be no opportunity for the Bill to be passed through all its stages within the necessary time. It was then that the telegram was despatched by Dr. White which is destined to become historic in the annals of the movement. "*House of Lords must meet Monday,*" was its brief but imperative summing up of the situation. It was a bold stroke characteristic of its author, but it speedily justified itself. The following evening a telegram reached the Lord High Commissioner (the Earl of Elgin) at the Palace of Holyroodhouse asking him to inform Dr. White, who was then at dinner at the Palace, that the House of Lords was to sit on the Monday to take the Third Reading of the Bill.

The result was that just before Dr. White rose to deliver his address at the close of the Assembly on the following Thursday, there was a dramatic and memorable incident. A telegram was handed to him, he opened it, glanced over its contents and then, remarking that it had been an eventful day, he read its contents as follows :

" Moderator, Assembly Hall, Edinburgh. Church of Scotland Bill received Royal Assent this afternoon. Under Secretary for Scotland."

The reading of this message so fraught with far-reaching issues, was followed by a demonstration of intense enthusiasm. It was the climax of a long and arduous struggle and it removed the last real obstacle in the path of Union.

Before this Assembly closed, an important task was committed to Dr. White. A number of laymen in the Church had made it possible for him to be entirely relieved of his own work in the Barony so that he might devote all his time to the prosecution of the Church Union movement and to a campaign on its behalf throughout the whole country. He was solemnly set apart for this special work, the whole Assembly standing while the Moderator addressed him and commended him in prayer. No such commission had ever before been given to any individual member ; it was significant of the dependence and trust with which the whole Assembly looked to Dr. White as its leader in the cause which he had brought so far successfully on its way, and which it now looked to him to carry to its complete fulfilment.

He entered at once on this special campaign. In pursuance of his commission to be, in Professor W. P. Paterson's vivid phrase, " the chief instrument and symbol " of Church Reunion in Scotland, he toiled incessantly and wandered far—from Kirkwall to Kelso, from Wick to Wigtown, from Lewis and Skye to Oban, to Aberdeen, Arbroath and Haddington, from South West to North East and the midlands between. Alike in public meetings and private conferences he achieved a notable piece of work. His public utterances often provoked open discussion which was recognised as being all to the good, while in his private conferences with Church Courts he was able to explain many minor points on which there had been confusion or misunderstanding, and thus remove difficulties out of the way. His readiness to receive suggestions which might be helpful in the final adjustment of the Plan of Union impressed even those who were not entirely favourable on certain points, while his complete mastery of the whole situation and calm confidence in the cause convinced the fainthearted, and his powerful speeches stirred even the apathetic. " He has done," it was said at the close of his campaign, " a work of inestimable value for which the two Churches more immediately concerned cannot be too grateful and for which all Scotland is his debtor."

In the next few years spent in the committees,

in the preparation of the steps for Union, Dr. White rendered invaluable service and established more than ever his ascendancy in his own Church, while his brethren in the United Free Church learned as fully to recognise and trust him as the leader in the whole movement.

The climax came when at the General Assembly of 1929 he rose to propose the final motion that the Assembly resolve upon an incorporating union with the United Free Church and pass into Standing Laws of the Church the overtures on Union so unanimously approved by the Presbyteries. It was felt to be a fateful occasion. Their Royal Highnesses the Duke and Duchess of York were in the Throne Gallery—the Duke being present officially as Lord High Commissioner—and there was a crowded and expectant House. The occasion was a great one for Dr. White himself as well as for the Assembly. It was no small honour to be standing at the Table at that momentous hour in the history of the Church as its recognised and trusted leader, and to have the privilege, at last, of taking the final steps on what had been a long and often difficult road.

In his opening words Dr. White acknowledged his personal indebtedness to Lord Sands for his helpful and loyal comradeship through the twenty years of negotiation, and he remarked that Lord Sands and himself in their Committee, and Principal Martin in the United Free Church Committee, were alone among those who had borne office from the beginning of the movement.

CHURCH UNION

"*Finis coronat opus. Magnum opus. Opera praeclara. . . . Te Deum laudamus*"—were the opening words of a speech which closed with a clarion call to the Church face to face with the future. The new day, he said, with its new needs called for a united and revitalised Church which would have the utmost freedom to grapple with the new situation, and an increased strength and efficiency to undertake the tasks that faced it. They did not expect the perfected mechanism to operate of its own accord. The message of Whitsunday had to be studied anew. They might be admirably equipped, but they were waiting the mighty, rushing wind, the irresistible impulse of God, the tongues of fire. There was a clear call to be unceasing in their prayer that He Who had so graciously guided them during the long years of negotiation would crown the happy issue with His blessing, that He would so sanctify them and confirm their faith that they might be fit instruments for His use, and that He would move mightily in His Church that His Kingdom in Scotland and throughout the world might be advanced.

It was a great speech—comprehensive and masterly in its survey, full of apt epigram, moving in its appeal, and delivered with a powerful and compelling eloquence. This last of many Church Union days in the Assembly had an impressive and memorable close. When the vote was taken and the whole House, save a small minority of three, rose in favour of Union there was an outburst of great enthusiasm. Cheering again and again renewed gave vent to the feelings of the members on the floor and of the public in the galleries. Then the Moderator offered a prayer of thanksgiving, at the close of which the Assembly broke into the Doxology, which was never sung with greater fervour or emotion.

It was a great day for the Church and for Scotland. And everyone felt how great a day it was for Dr. White. He had seen at last the end for which through long years he had lived and laboured; and as he stood there, the leading figure in the historic scene, many wondered what conflicting emotions were surging beneath his strong, calm exterior in the hour of his triumph.

The climax came at a meeting of the joint committees of the two churches held on June 14, 1929, when Dr. White was chosen to be the first Moderator of the United Assembly. His nomination, proposed by Principal Martin of the United Free Church, and seconded by Professor W. P. Paterson of the Church of Scotland, was carried with acclamation. This was followed by the conferment of the honorary degree of L.L.D. of Edinburgh University, and later, by the announcement that he would be presented with the Freedom of the City.

CHAPTER XIII

THE   ECCLESIASTIC

THE popular conception of Dr. White is undoubt-edly that of a great ecclesiastic.   In an age when great ecclesiastics are said to be steadily dis-appearing he has remained almost the sole representative of what was once a famous race in Scotland.

But there are ecclesiastics and ecclesiastics. The late Sir William Robertson Nicoll used to tell of a friend of his who was accustomed to enumerate the qualifications necessary for ecclesi-astical supremacy.   According to this authority, the man who would shine as an ecclesiastic must have the art of clearing his throat in a lengthened and impressive manner ;   he must know how to use large gold eye-glasses, moving them up and down solemnly to the march of his speech and laying them to rest where his delighted hearers might gaze upon them.   He must be a master of such sonorous phrases as " I desire to associate myself."   He must suppress his own personality, his own quickness, his own cleverness.   To be a great ecclesiastic, according to this authority, an able man must rigidly suppress his ability, a humorous man his humour and a sarcastic man his sarcasm.

DR. JOHN WHITE

To such a type of ecclesiastic Dr. White certainly does not belong. There is nothing ponderous or formal or official about him. He represents not the old race of ecclesiastic but the new. With all the dignity which seems so natural to a man of his noble presence, he is at the same time full of a restless activity and energy and palpitating with life to his finger tips. Never has he sought to repress his natural gifts because of the position he has occupied. Time and again has the Assembly marvelled at his quickness and cleverness, while his humour has often enlivened a dull sitting and even his sarcasm, though sparingly used, has sometimes flashed like lightning in a sultry atmosphere.

As he sits in his place as leader of the General Assembly he makes an interesting study. There, in the seats of the mighty, he follows in a noble succession. And yet it may well be questioned if any leader within living memory—or indeed any leader at any time in the history of the Assembly—ever fitted more perfectly into the position. For this place it might almost seem had this man been born.

The leader of the General Assembly has even more responsibility for the whole conduct of its affairs than the leader of the House of Commons for the business of that House. To quote Lord Sands, who may be accepted as an authority—" He is expected to take the initiative in all motions of ceremony or courtesy, and what is more important, to keep his eye and his hand upon the substance of the business, to guide and to steady the Assembly, to see the bearing of a proposal upon other branches of Church work, and to resist the rash, ill-considered motions which sometimes catch the ear of a popular Assembly. There is obvious and great advantage in the constant presence and vigilance of a leader whose duty it is to keep his eyes upon every matter before the Assembly, and who can intervene if necessary with some authority and without the reproach of always meddling. . . . He must watch all the business whether he is interested in it or not. He must read every report that is coming up and, in particular, every proposed deliverance. He must be on the alert to prevent the acceptance without full understanding of any proposal which seems to him injudicious, to conflict with precedent, or to embarrass some other department of work by overlapping or otherwise ; he must be ready with suggestions for the reconciliation of motions and the avoidance of division ; he must guard the purse-strings and he must never hesitate to intervene, as an ordinary member may hesitate as to whether to speak or not."

There have been leaders of Assembly who have had neither the natural aptitude nor the training for this kind of thing. Unfitted for the mastery of details and unconcerned as to the course of business so long as there arose no glaring confusion or crisis, they were content to let matters drift and take care of themselves.

There have been other leaders who never slackened their grip of affairs, but were always on the alert and ready for every emergency.

No one ever more quickly adapted himself to the requirements than Dr. White, or more speedily secured complete authority in the Assembly. The criticism has indeed been levelled against him that his domination has been too great. The masterfulness of his disposition has sometimes been apparent, and he may have been inclined at times to ride rough shod over opposition or obstruction with which he was manifestly impatient. Yet a mellowing process had been going on before he attained to leadership, and it has been still more pronounced since then. He can keep a firm grip of himself, and at times can even contrive to suffer fools gladly for the sake of any cause he has at heart. He knows how to be conciliatory without any sacrifice of principle.

One conspicuous feature in Dr. White's leadership of the Assembly has been his alertness. Nothing seems to escape him ; he requires no prompting from officials round the Table, but is always the first to sense a situation and seize the opportunity for a helpful intervention. To be ready to " jump up " when " anything threatens to go agley " has been said to be one of the prime requisites of an Assembly leader. Dr. White is an adept at " jumping up." To have seen him spring to his feet, like a Captain rushing to take the wheel in an anxious moment, is something to be remembered. Many have marvelled at the readiness and resource with which on such occasions he has taken command, and the quickness with which the Assembly has responded to his firm, sure hand of control.

It would be an entire mistake, however, to suppose that he always takes the middle course or makes his motto "safety first." Notable instances might, of course, be quoted of how he has been able, by the drafting of a new motion, to bring apparently irreconcilable proposals into unison and to secure unanimity on some subject on which the assembly threatened to be hopelessly and perhaps dangerously divided. But his reputation is not that of the astute and crafty ecclesiastic of tradition, whose powers of mystification were such that a double meaning could be taken out of everything he said. It used to be remarked, half in jest and half in earnest, by his enemies that "Principal Rainy was misty as well as Rainy." This is not the tendency of Dr. White. It is easier for him, and more natural, to be downright and forthright even if it means running a risk. There have been times when he has seemed to risk everything on some bold avowal, on some uncompromising stand, when a weaker man would have sought a *via media*. On such occasions the masterfulness of the man, which at other times may have threatened to be his weakness, has proved to be his strength. He has shown that he can conquer as well as conciliate.

It was said of a great ecclesiastic of the past

that in any deliberative assembly in the world he would have taken the same place as in the Assembly. If he had been a member of the House of Commons he would most certainly have been the first man there and it would have been so in the House of Lords or anywhere else. The words were never truer than in their application to Dr. White. And, whatever may be the changes in the General Assembly brought about by the Union of the Churches, it may safely be predicted that it will not matter much where Dr. White sits for, wherever he is, there will be the head of the Table.

But it is not in the Assembly only that Dr. White has proved himself a great ecclesiastic and a born leader. He has taken the same position in the general ecclesiastical life of Scotland. One instance may be found in connection with his work on the Scottish Churches Council, with the formation of which he had much to do, and of which he was President for the first three years of its existence. The Council, composed of representatives of the Church of Scotland, United Free Church, Episcopal Church in Scotland, Congregationalists, Baptists, Wesleyan Methodists, Primitive Methodists, Reformed Presbyterians, and Original Secession, was formed for the purpose of giving effective expression to Christian opinion in Scotland on urgent matters, and for taking common action for the Christian good of Scotland and the world. Dr. White became by common consent the leader as well as the

President of the Council, and guided its deliberations with a tact, wisdom and statesmanship which called forth the admiration of the representatives of all the constituent Churches.

The supreme example, however, of Dr. White's leadership of all the Churches in Scotland has been supplied in connection with the controversy in regard to the question of religious instruction in Schools as affected by the Local Government Bill for Scotland of 1929. He was the first to apprehend the danger in the proposed legislation and when the Churches awoke to the gravity of the situation they all turned instinctively to him as the leader on whom they could rely and whom without hesitation they could follow.

His work in that connection overshadowed for a time even his labours for Church Union. Never in all his public work had his skill in negotiation, his persistence in advocacy, or his readiness and resource in conference, been more conspicuously displayed. In important interviews both in Edinburgh and in London, with the Secretary of State for Scotland and officials of the Education Department, he urged the claim of the Protestant Churches of Scotland for the safeguarding of religious instruction in the schools with a force and power difficult to resist. His mastery of the situation, and the relentless logic with which he pursued his case, made him a formidable figure in official circles. Time and again he journeyed to London, sometimes alone, and at others supported by representatives of the various Churches, resolved to leave no stone unturned in order to secure a satisfactory arrangement. No campaign was ever conducted with a greater determination or a more complete unanimity on the part of the Churches.

An eminent Churchman, speaking in the Church of Scotland Assembly of 1929, told of a certain occasion when Dr. White was in London in connection with this question and matters had come to a deadlock. The Government officials had finally intimated that such a clause in the Bill as had been demanded could not be drafted. It seemed the last word had been said, but they reckoned without Dr. White. According to this Churchman, who was on the spot and personally familiar with the circumstances, Dr. White sat up all that night, and before morning had drafted a clause which the Government official said could not be drafted. Next day he was early at the House of Commons and secured the approval, first of the Unionist members and then of the Labour members, and so ensured the safe passage of the Bill as thus amended. It was a triumph of skill and diplomacy.

The controversy had been a long and anxious one, involving quite an unusual expenditure of time and strength. While it had been found impossible to secure all that had been demanded, yet it was felt that such concessions were obtained from the Government as would give the teaching of the Bible in the schools a position of security as great as, if not greater than, it had possessed since

1872, and thus maintain the tradition of religious education so dear to every truly Scottish heart. Dr. White's great services were gratefully recognised by all the Churches both in their Supreme Courts and otherwise. Notwithstanding all that he had done in the cause of Church Union, it has been said by those most intimate with the difficulties in connection with the problem of religious instruction that his achievement in this matter may be found in the long run to be the greatest thing he has done for his native land.

An ecclesiastic of the first rank, and a Church leader, Dr. White has certainly proved himself to be, and a man of vision with an unusual grasp of affairs, a strong practical mind and an extraordinary mastery of details. But that is not all. More and more with the passing years he has revealed his possession of the qualities of true statesmanship. There are those who have declared that he will eventually stand higher in the roll of fame than either Rainy or Chalmers, and that his constructive work for the Church in Scotland will be found to be the greatest since that accomplished by Carstares at the Revolution Settlement in the seventeenth century.

It is too soon, however, to attempt to assess the place which John White will hold in history, for his work is not yet done. In the years that lie ahead after the Union of the Churches, with all the difficult and delicate, yet necessary, readjustments Union has entailed, there will be more need than ever of his wise, strong, guiding hand.

And as he is still in the full vigour of his manhood with all his powers at their best, his future may be as rich in achievement as his past.

This chapter may fittingly conclude with appreciations of Dr. White by three well-known men who have been associated with him at different stages in his career. The Right Hon. Sir Robert Horne, M.P., an old fellow student, writes :

" In view of my very long and affectionate friendship with Dr. White, I would have been very glad to do what you ask in making a contribution to the book you are writing about him. My memories of him are many and pleasant, and the admiration in which he is held by the whole of Scotland at the present time is the sequel to a sentiment which most of us who were his fellow students cherished when we were at College together. The great work which he has done in helping to bring the Churches of Scotland into one united Communion will stand out in the future as one of the greatest achievements of our time ; and I am sure you are doing the public life of Scotland a service in making clear to our people the qualities of character and capacity—industry and devotion to duty—which make John White one of the great and notable figures of our time. If I had had time I would gladly have expanded these short observations, and I could have spent happy hours in recalling interesting episodes in Dr. White's life, both as a student and as a minister, in which he and

I have been mutually concerned. But the claims of many activities are too exacting to allow me this privilege, and I must content myself with wishing you every success in the task which you have undertaken to present to the world a suitable biography of my old friend."

Another fellow student, Professor Ernest F. Scott, of New York, whose reminiscences of student days have been given in a former chapter adds this reference to Dr. White as an ecclesiastical leader :

" I was well aware that John White would some day be a distinguished figure, but I always thought of him as making his mark as a philosophical thinker. It came to me with something like a shock many years afterwards, when I had long been on the other side of the Atlantic, to learn that he had become a great ecclesiastical leader. But I can now see that he had always the two sides to his nature— the gift for abstract speculation and the gift for action. It is fortunate for Scotland at this time that a leader has appeared with this rare combination of powers. For the last half century we have been dreaming of a union of churches, but few could ever think of it as anything but an impossible ideal. What we needed was the man of wide outlook and firm grasp of ultimate principles who at the same time had the force to realise his thought in action."

The other appreciation is by the Rev. Dr. Archibald Fleming, the distinguished minister of St. Columba's (Church of Scotland), Pont Street, London, who has been associated with Dr. White in the later stages of his career. Dr. Fleming writes :

" It is only because, living out of Scotland, one may perhaps be able to take a more detached view of Scottish affairs and personalities—a view less ruffled by nearer detail—that, on urgent request, I hazard a partial appreciation of my distinguished friend, Dr. John White.

" His personality first loomed on my horizon ere I knew him personally ; it was an impressionist and hearsay projection, as it were, of a young and eager minister at Shettleston, to whom work was play, and difficulties were made to be overcome, and to whom to be parish minister meant being minister of the parish, and not a mere figurehead.

" Then one heard of him as a growing power in the largest Presbytery of the Church ; original and definite in his opinions and policies ; glad to have friends but not afraid of encountering opponents when the alternative to doing so was that of dropping a sound scheme merely because it proved *prima facie* unpopular. Later still, one got to recognize forcefulness controlled and directed by growing experience, and the faculty for leadership taking on the rarer qualities of statesmanship. One could see in him the growing instinct for big things, and a flair for the discovery of key positions.

" By these gifts he came to discover the two great issues in Scotland : the bringing of the Church into direct contact with the needs and aspirations, secular as well as spiritual, of the people—out of this the Committee on Church and Nation grew ; and the inevitability of a measure of Church Union in Scotland if there were not to be, sooner or later, an ecclesiastical debacle.

" Cognate to these large problems, was that of education ; for a Church wholly given to the highest interests of the people could only conserve the traditional alliance of religion and schooling in Scotland by presenting against schemes of secularization an unbroken front. His preoccupation with these great issues inevitably made John White an Assembly man : a Church Union leader : and, in the prime of his powers, the chief intermediary between the Scottish Churches and Parliament.

" It was on this last arena that his full intellectual stature was revealed.   In these recent years he has been frequently in London.   He has done me the honour of discussing with me most of the highly important questions which brought him on successive missions to White-hall.   Sedulously he attended, day by day, in the Scottish Grand Committee Room of the House of Commons, when Scottish Church legislation was afoot.   Neither cleric nor parliamentarian outrivalled him in minute knowledge of the proposed enactments and their subtle implications. His statesmanship and easy mastery of the subject were universally acknowledged. His advice was more and more trusted, his disinterested patriotism and honesty on all sides recognized. Had Dr. White chosen Law as his profession, there would have been in the long run but one place for him, namely, at the top.

"It has been inevitable that John White should make enemies as well as friends. He is too downright to be uniformly conciliatory ; too convinced to be patient of half measures. But those who know him best love him most. They know his gentleness and tenderheartedness ; his reliability ; his love of Nature and of manly sport ; his zeal for God, Kirk, and King ; his lion heart when things are adverse. John White is a great asset to Scotland ; and he is a great asset to a friend."

CHAPTER XIV

THE MAN

THE closing words of Dr. Fleming's tribute indicate that there is another side to Dr. White than that which seems to bulk most largely in the public mind. It is well ; it is, indeed, only fair and just, that the other side should be revealed.

It may be at once admitted that, in the eyes of many who do not know him, the strength of Dr. White seems to overshadow all his other qualities. They look upon him as a strong, cold, hard man, so determined and forceful in his personality as to be ruthless in the pursuit of his purpose and devoid alike of the more human qualities of sympathy, humour and tenderness. Never was a popular impression farther from the truth. There may be about him an aspect of severity, and a coldness on the surface. But nature sometimes covers an unusually fine spirit with a cloak of severity for its protection, and this is very true of Dr. White. One of those best qualified to form an impression writes : " No man of all the men of my time has been more the ' lame dog's ' friend than White has. He is always helping those ' lame dogs over stiles.' That practical turn in his nature will not allow him only to express sympathy ; he must *do* something."

In his student days the human side of John White was known to his fellows and then, when he might have been in danger of outgrowing it in the stress of affairs, another influence came into his life. " The danger for any man of John White's ability and force," writes one who saw behind the scenes, " was that he should be scornful ; the salvation of such a man is that he should have, early enough in life, some influence strong enough to hold him and tender enough to sweeten him." That influence, the writer goes on to say, came with Mrs. White, and here we have revealed one of the secrets of the real success of a great career.

From his marriage on September 5, 1893, to Miss Margaret Gardner, eldest daughter of Mr. John Gardner, Muirpark, Partick, Dr. White's home life has been a singularly happy one. Mrs. White has meant far more to him than is conveyed in the formal phrase of " a worthy helpmeet." Their family circle has radiated a brightness in which many others have shared. A former assistant, the Rev. David Scott, B.D., now of Montreal, writes of the Sunday evenings when " Dr. White discussed plans of work and invited the opinions of the young men, and at others turned the talk on some of the great Church schemes in which he was engaged until they felt in the presence of some great creative artificer who was successfully turning the most obdurate and unmalleable material to give expression to his vision."

But Mr. Scott has also described other Sunday evenings, " when at the close of a strenuous day the Moderator's study was filled with a heterogeneous crowd, comprising assistants, daughters, sons, a " wheen " of their school friends, and in the midst Dr. and Mrs. White. Those who looked then for the awe-inspiring Apostle looked in vain. He had with joyful ease shed that character and was a boy among his boys, giving and taking schoolboy chaff, and leaving one with the impression that, in his opinion, the biggest thing that had been done all the week was the ' converting of that try at Anniesland ' the day before."

The reference to the games at Anniesland is a reminder of Dr. White's interest in sport and of the fact that among all his distinctions he is, perhaps, prouder of none than of being the father of two such noted Rugby footballers as Mr. M. K. White, Secretary of the West of Scotland Club, and Mr. J. G. White, Cambridge Blue, Captain of the Glasgow Academicals and a brilliant " forward."

Dr. White's own favourite sport is salmon fishing. When he can lay aside the cares of Church and State he is usually found by the side of some river plying the rod, not as an amateur but as one trained in the art, and as if it were the supreme interest of his life. He has fished in many parts of the country—the Duke of Buccleuch said he never knew that " a learned and holy

M

Moderator could be a good fisherman in the
mundane sense " until Dr. White had been on
some of his waters—but Speyside has specially
fascinated him.   He has returned more than once
to spend his holiday in that district, and it has been
said that when he was not immersed in Church
affairs he was invariably to be found on the
banks of the Spey.   In the days before motor
cars came into general use he would often be
seen cycling in the country, and the story is still
told of an experience he once had in Strathspey.
He had left his bicycle on a bridge near Grantown
and gone up the river fishing.   When he returned after an hour or two the bicycle was gone,
and it has never been heard of since.

   Dr. White would frequently share the contents
of his basket with his friends and a gift of salmon
sent to the late Rev. Dr. Donald Macleod, of the
Park Church, Glasgow, who was then residing
in retirement in Edinburgh, brought two letters
highly characteristic of the genial pen of the
editor of *Good Words*:

             " 8, TIPPERLIN ROAD,
                   " EDINBURGH,
                      "*February* 16, 1912.

" MY DEAR WHITE,
   " Good gracious ! Such a fish ! Such a big
fish for Mrs. Macleod and me ! ! You must
have poached it, or got one to play it for you—for
you never could have caught it yourself.   More
likely it was your clever wife.   But in Glen

Morriston, that glorious glen ! How did you get into Paradise ? Without Gaelic too. It is incredible.

"My dear fellow, you and Mrs. White are gloriously kind and I do not know whether we love you both or the fish most. At all events we shall have a fish with a dram in its honour and to both your healths—two drams !

"A thousand thanks to both of you.

" . . . I am addressing this letter to Glasgow as I am sure you will not desert the Barony for the sake of hearing the minister of Glen Morriston.

"God Bless you.

"Yours affectionately and your wife's also,
"(*Signed*) DONALD MACLEOD."

"8, TIPPERLIN ROAD,
"EDINBURGH,
"*February* 17, 1912.

"MY DEAR WHITE,

"Believing that you were too devoted to the Barony pulpit to exchange it for a Highland glen where only Gaelic is spoken, and where the only attraction is the more glorious scenery than in the High Street of Glasgow and bigger game to be caught than even your big congregation, I addressed my thanks to Mrs. White and yourself to Glasgow, but I find your spirit of sport is too strong for you and so I write this to Glen Morriston by express in order to be sure that you will get it—my most hearty thanks for your magnificent cut of salmon. You will probably get the letter I sent to Glasgow as well, and you can therefore judge the strength of my gratitude.

"That you ever killed the salmon seems to me highly improbable—for it must have been at the least a 20 lb. fish—and where could you have ever learned the skill to tackle such a fellow? No doubt you had a gillie to whom you handed the rod and half a crown to hold his tongue afterwards, but I will get the truth from Mrs. White.

"Man, I envy you or rather I *hate* you—such is my jealousy! Glen Morriston alone should have been enough for a town-bred laddie, for it is a glorious glen, and to have some days there would be reward enough for any man with an eye to see and a heart to feel its inspiration.

"What a change from the Presbytery of Glasgow and the toil of the Barony! How did you manage it? You must be a clever fellow after all and almost fit for the Junior Clerkship.

"Mrs. Macleod sends grateful love to Mrs. White and yourself.

"God bless you both,
            "Yours ever,
                    "(*Signed*) DONALD MACLEOD."

Reference has been made to the manner in which Dr White can relax in the family circle. But he can also do so in any congenial company, and at a social function there are few men who can give more vivacity to the proceedings. As an after-dinner speaker he excels, with his flashing epigrams, his racy humour and his vigorous yet easy eloquence. Among many notable appearances he has made on public occasions of the kind, one stands out conspicuously as an example of his versatility.

It was a banquet in the Glasgow Trades House given by the Hammermen Incorporation, and one of the most brilliant functions of its kind. On that evening, Wednesday, October 14, 1925, Glasgow was said to have re-established its reputation for postprandial oratory, and although the distinguished list of speakers included Viscount Ullswater, the Ex-Speaker of the House of Commons, it was acknowledged on all hands that the feature of the occasion was the speech delivered by Dr. White. It kept the company in ripples of laughter with its sparkling wit, which came to a climax in the verse with which he concluded.

There had been entrusted to him the toast of the evening, " The Trades House and Deacon Convener," and he confessed he had a great admiration for the temerity—he might almost say courage—which induced them to ask a clergyman to propose the toast of the evening, despite all recent criticism of their sermons as being dull, flat and unprofitable. " I do not expect you," he said, " to range yourselves alongside Margot, Countess of Oxford and Asquith, who has been supporting the attack on sermons because less concerned about the love of God than the lack of love in man. One can but note her objection and sympathise with her forlorn state through the lack of love in man." Dean Inge next received attention with the remark that, "we need one gloomy Dean to give edge to our thinking but I don't think we could stand two."

Referring specially to the Hammermen Incorporation, under whose auspices they were met, he remarked that if they had smashed James Watt's engine—or prevented his kettle from boiling—they might have rescued our national life and kept one plank out of the Liberal platform. That steam engine had altered the whole face of social life and made it chiefly urban. Man was not made to be a cog in a great industrial mechanism, and there they had the psychological cause of so much unrest.

That led logically to the cry, "Back to the land," but not being a politician he was not going to advocate or criticise Mr. Lloyd George's land policy. He was not sure that he understood it any better than the Liberal Conference at Inverness had understood the Church Union question which a few members discussed without any prejudice arising from a knowledge of the facts. However alluring might be the cry "Back to the Land," he was not sure that many of them were over anxious to take up allotments. Then he pictured Mr. Lloyd George after his many speeches returning from the North, humming very quietly but very contentedly in the corner of a first-class smoker—with the Presbyterian mixture —the well known lines, "well," he added,

" perhaps not well known and possibly not even
lines:

> " Give me the sparkling Strand
> Looking by night so grand,
> Give me a Savoy band
> In shine or rain.

> " Lunch at the A.B.C.
> Steamboats and L.C.C.,
> Country folk envy me
> Me and my Jane."

" Tune ' London New,' " he added amid the
uproarious laughter with which this sally was
greeted.

In private life, Dr. White is one of the most
companionable of men. He loves his pipe and
in a friendly talk around the fireside he can
unbend delightfully. As a smoker he is almost
as well known as Mr. Baldwin. There is, indeed,
a tobacco which bears his name, a rare distinction
even for a public man. Specially prepared (by
a firm of Glasgow tobacconists) and sold as
" Dr. White's Glasgow Presbyterian Mixture,"
it is now well known all over the world.

The story of this cannot be omitted in any
record of Dr. White's life. He has himself
admitted that it is one of his " claims to fame,"
although he merrily added, " I am sorry to say
it always ends in smoke ! "

The mixture had been originally introduced
to Dr. White by a friend in South Africa. He

made some improvements of his own and got
his tobacconist to prepare a special blend which
he has used ever since. One day Sir Robert
Bruce, Editor of the *Glasgow Herald* got a
pipeful from Dr. White, and when Sir Robert was
on a visit to Viscount Haldane, he gave him
some of the tobacco. Lord Haldane immediately said, " I must take this to Mr. Baldwin,"
with the result that Mr. Baldwin some years
later specially mentioned the " Presbyterian
Mixture " in course of a speech at Dundee. There
is now an extensive trade in the tobacco, in tins
stamped with Dr. White's name and Mr.
Baldwin's.

The rich humanity of Dr. White was nowhere
more strikingly in evidence than on the battle-
field. As a Chaplain with the Cameronians he
won the undying admiration and gratitude of
the soldiers whom he served. Men not given
to flattery were so impressed by a Padre who
was utterly regardless of danger where duty called
him, who was ready to turn his hand to anything
however menial in the way of service, and whose
personality had in it such elements both of
strength and of real human tenderness, that they
were moved to write home about him in unres-
trained terms. No finer tributes could ever be
paid.

A Glasgow man in a letter to his friends
wrote : " Mr. White is the heart and soul of
all our gatherings, and no one ever feels downcast
when he is there. He is always trying to help

someone, and if I'm spared to come home again I'm going to join the Barony Church and sit under one of the best and truest men I ever met."

" You never saw a man getting through so much work in a day," wrote one of the wounded, " as our Chaplain did on 20th July, when we were in the big advance. He was here, there, and everywhere, regardless of danger, thinking only of what he could do for us. With tunic off, and sleeves rolled up he moved about, bandaging an arm or a leg or a head, and cheering everyone with his jokes and remarks. When he had placed a wounded man on a stretcher he would put a cigarette in the man's mouth, light it for him and see him safely off to the rear. Yon's the kind of man we need out here and the 5th S.R. are lucky to have him."

" Did you see Mr. White out at the front ? " another of the wounded was asked. " I should think I did see Mr. White," was the reply. " After I was wounded he carried me on his back more than a mile to the dressing station, only stopping three times on the way, and that was to supply me with a new cigarette."

When the war was over and the men returned home they did not forget Dr. White and the Barony. A link had been forged that was to remain. And even men at a distance would beg their old Padre to do them the honour of baptising a child or ask him to render them some other service, and to no such request did Dr. White ever turn a deaf ear. In intimate converse with the highest in the land, he has remained at the same time the friend of the common people.

Dr. White has spent much of his life in the fierce glare of publicity, but some of his best deeds have been done behind the scenes. A prodigious worker, with every hour of the day—and often far into the night—spent in unceasing toil, he has been able somehow to find time to perform many of those " little nameless, unremembered acts of kindness and of love " which impart a radiance to life. In addition to the cares of his own people he has carried in a sense the cares of all the Churches, and instances could be told of ministers, some of them in obscure places, who treasure letters from Dr. White which brought them encouragement and new hope at times when they were inclined to feel that nobody thought about them or knew anything of their work.

It has been a marvel to many how Dr. White gets through all his work. The secret lies not only in intense industry but also in great capacity. He is a quick worker. At the head of a great business he would have been a striking success. One of his most intimate friends from early days until now, in referring to " the forcefulness of his personality and his superior mental powers," writes : " He always seemed to see further and to know better what to do than most men, and he knew how to set about doing it. One feature always characteristic of him has been his extraordinary calmness. Situations which would be upsetting to ordinary men never seemed to perturb him in the least."

Dr. White's strict regard for accuracy has become a legend. On one occasion, in writing to the late Lord Balfour of Burleigh, he used a wrong date which brought from his lordship an amusing letter chaffing him on " the first and only error he had known," and concluding in the same spirit, " But I am really your warm friend, *as always*, B. of B."

It has often been remarked of Dr. White that he can adapt himself to any company. That a man of his personality should find himself at home among men of affairs, whether of Church or State, is not surprising. He would always be able to hold his own with the best of them. But it does not follow as a matter of course— indeed rather the reverse—that a man of this type should be able to make friends readily with young people. Yet this Dr. White has actually done. Young men and women soon find something about him which, instead of repelling by its severity, draws them by its geniality. As one young man put it, " there is a splendid sincerity about him and never any cant." Without any sacrifice of principle or compromise of personality he can mix with young folk like one of themselves.

The most severe test, however, is that of little children, with their unfailing instinct and their strong likes and dislikes, and it has been a revelation, as Dr. White has gone on his tours of visitation throughout the country, to see how the children of the manses have responded to him. Somewhat overawed at first by the august visitor, they soon intuitively realised that they had found a friend, and before long were clustering round him and climbing on his knee. " A fine man with the bairns," is a saying with a world of meaning and significance behind it.

It was once said that no phrase could be more aptly applied to John White than what Emerson calls Clarendon's " electric torch," in his description of Hampden : " He was of an industry and vigilance not to be tired out or wearied by the most laborious, and of parts not to be imposed on by the most subtle and sharp, and of a personal courage equal to his best parts."

And yet there is something more. Behind both the ecclesiastic and the man there is the Christian. It is the strong, deep Christian faith of Dr. White that has made him what he is, and enabled him to do what he has done, and this the Church of the future in Scotland will discover more and more as time goes on. What that future may still hold in store for him it would be impossible to forecast. This much, however, is assured. As it has been said of other great men, so it may be said of him, that whether he speaks or is silent it will be impossible to be indifferent to him. His personality will always make itself felt.

INDEX

INDEX

INDEX

THE LONDON AND NORWICH PRESS, LIMITED, ST. GILES WORKS, NORWICH